WEAPON

WEAPONS OF THE US SPECIAL OPERATIONS COMMAND

CHRIS McNAB
Series Editor Martin Pegler

Illustrated by Johnny Shumate & Alan Gilliland

OSPREY PUBLISHING
Bloomsbury Publishing Plc

Kemp House, Chawley Park, Oxford OX2 9PH, UK
29 Earlsfort Terrace, Dublin 2, Ireland
1385 Broadway, 5th Floor, New York, NY 10018, USA
Email: info@ospreypublishing.com
www.ospreypublishing.com

First published in Great Britain in 2019
Transferred to digital print in 2022

A catalog record for this book is available from the British Library.

Print ISBN: 978 1 4728 3309 9
ePub: 978 1 4728 3310 5
ePDF: 978 1 4728 3308 2
XML: 978 1 4728 3311 2

Index by Rob Munro
Typeset by PDQ Digital Media Solutions, Bungay, UK
Printed and bound in India by Replika Press Private Ltd.

24 25 26 27 28 10 9 8 7 6 5 4

The Woodland Trust
Osprey Publishing supports the Woodland Trust, the UK's leading woodland conservation charity.

www.ospreypublishing.com
To find out more about our authors and books visit our website. Here you will find extracts, author interviews, details of forthcoming events and the option to sign-up for our newsletter.

Acknowledgments
Thanks go to Nick Reynolds at Osprey for his editorial support and project management of this work, and also to illustrators Johnny Shumate and Alan Gilliland for their customary fine artworks.

Editor's note
In this book linear, weight, and volume measurements are given in US customary units of measurement (yards, feet, inches, pounds, grains). The exception is weapons caliber, where metric is used in many cases, depending on the context. The US military habitually uses metric for distances and weapon ranges. Conversions from metric into US customary are given in the text for clarity.

Image acknowledgments
Front cover, above: The M110 Semi Automatic Sniper System (SASS) commands ranges of up to and even exceeding 800m (875yd). Modern semi-auto sniper systems have become the equal in accuracy of many bolt-action types. (Photo Courtesy of PEO Soldier/Wikimedia/ Public Domain)

Front cover, below: A US SOF soldier readies his Mk 20 Sniper Support Rifle (SSR), a sniper version of the FN SCAR-H, on a hilltop near Nawa Garay village, Kajran District, Day Kundi Province, Afghanistan, April 3, 2012. (Mass Communication Specialist 2d Class Jacob L. Dillon via NATO Training Mission Afghanistan/Wikimedia/ Public Domain)

Title-page image: A Pararescueman with the 33d Expeditionary Rescue Squadron fires a Mk 14 Enhanced Battle Rifle (EBR). The scope is a Leupold Mk 4 3.5–10×, ideal for battlefield sniping at ranges of 200–1,000m (219–1,094yd). (US Air Force photo by Staff Sgt Christopher Boitz)

The Royal Armouries
The Royal Armouries is Britain's national museum of arms and armour, and one of the most important museums of its type in the world. Its origins lie in the Middle Ages, and at its core is the celebrated collection originating in the nation's working arsenal, assembled over many centuries at the Tower of London. In the reign of Elizabeth I, selected items began to be arranged for display to visitors, making the Royal Armouries heir to one of the oldest deliberately created visitor attractions in the country. The collection is now housed and displayed at three sites: the White Tower at the Tower of London, a purpose-built museum in Leeds, and Fort Nelson near Portsmouth. To find out more, explore online at: collections.royalarmouries.org

CONTENTS

INTRODUCTION

The United States Special Operations Command (USSOCOM or SOCOM) was formally established on April 13, 1987 and activated three days later under the command of General James J. Lindsay following a long period of self-analysis by the United States Special Operations Forces (SOF) community, triggered by the disastrous outcome of the failed Operation *Eagle Claw* hostage-rescue mission in Iran on April 24, 1980. SOCOM's role was to be a broad one: to oversee and harmonize all US SOF activities. SOCOM was therefore to be in the vanguard of future US military operations.

We should be careful, however, to recognize that SOCOM is a particularly broad church, with a diverse range of SOF units and formations under its purview, all with their own specific tactical strengths and operational remits. They range from the large-scale and the familiar, such as the US Army's Special Forces (the "Green Berets") and 75th Ranger Regiment, and the US Navy's SEALs, down to smaller and more secretive units, of which the 1st Special Forces Operational Detachment-Delta (Airborne), otherwise known as "Delta Force," is a supreme example. Each of the four major US services – Army, Navy, Marine Corps, and Air Force – has a Special Operations Command (SOC) governing its SOF units and activities, plus a Joint Special Operations Command (JSOC) providing, by its own definition, "a joint headquarters designed to study special operations requirements and techniques; ensure interoperability and equipment standardization; plan and conduct joint special operations exercises and training; and develop joint special operations tactics." JSOC itself includes Delta Force and the Naval Special Warfare Development Group (DEVGRU), the latter otherwise known as SEAL Team Six.

Since the formation of US special forces during World War II, the operational remit of US SOF, taken collectively, has become both broad and demanding. Mission types include high-risk reconnaissance,

counterterrorism, hostage rescue, psychological warfare, cyber and unconventional warfare, civil affairs, training foreign armies, counternarcotics, and direct-action. Although SOCOM operators have performed and continue to perform all these roles, since 2001 it is direct-action that has dominated much of the operational remit. Direct-action missions are defined by the US Department of Defense as:

> Short-duration strikes and other small-scale offensive actions conducted as a special operation in hostile, denied, or politically sensitive environments and which employ specialized military capabilities to seize, destroy, capture, exploit, recover, or damage designated targets. Direct action differs from conventional offensive actions in the level of physical and political risk, operational techniques, and the degree of discriminate and precise use of force to achieve specific objectives. (Department of Defense 2009: 163)

Primarily in Iraq and Afghanistan, but also on numerous other front lines in the "War on Terror," SOF soldiers have expended millions of rounds of ammunition in high-risk offensive operations against both conventional forces and insurgents. Although these missions have often enjoyed the earth-shaking support of air strikes and, if available and within range, artillery fire, they have frequently been decided by personal firepower alone at relatively close ranges. In such environments, small arms reign supreme.

ABOVE LEFT
Taken in 1987, this photograph shows a Navy SEAL with a Colt Commando or XM177. The Commando was a primary SOF weapon in the Vietnam War, and was replaced in the 1990s by the M4 Carbine. (PH1 CHUCK MUSS/ Wikimedia/Public Domain)

ABOVE RIGHT
US Army Special Forces soldiers of the 3d Special Forces Group (Airborne) practice room-clearing techniques. Note the substantial size of the foregrip on their M4A1 Carbines; some foregrip types, such as the GPSI Grip Pod, include extendable bipod legs. (US Army photo by Sgt Matthew S. Friberg)

Clearly demonstrating his weapon's over-the-beach (OTB) rating, this US Navy SEAL combat swimmer is armed with a Mk 17 Mod 0 SCAR-H (Special Operations Forces Combat Assault Rifle – Heavy) equipped with an EOTech sight. (US DoD)

Since 2001 and the beginning of the "War on Terror," SOCOM's operational commitments have highlighted the quality of its firearms, and the rationale behind their selection, to the extreme. The pressure-testing has forced SOCOM units to think carefully about what their needs are as front-line fighting forces. Some of the requirements are both universal and constant. Every soldier wants a rifle or handgun that is reliable (a quality that is valued above all others), powerful, accurate, and user-friendly. Yet what has entered the equation in SOCOM is the quality of *adaptability*. For SOF troops, mission parameters can vary tremendously from day to day, even hour to hour, and their firearms need to reflect that reality. For example, one day a SOF unit might be charged with neutralizing an individual high-value target (HVT) within a complex urban environment, with the likelihood of having to engage multiple targets rapidly in close-quarters battle (CQB). The next day, by contrast, the unit might be deployed on a direct-action mission against an enemy training camp in a remote mountainous region, where the engagement ranges may stretch to hundreds of meters. To meet both requirements, and all the shades and hues in between, SOF soldiers need either a range of weapon types from which to select the appropriate firearm, or a single modular type that can be adapted either through the addition of mission-specific accessories (suppressors, optical sights, tactical lights, etc.) or through physical reconfiguration (e.g. changing the receiver, barrel, caliber, forend, or stock). The result is in effect a weapons "family" within a single weapon, one that can be configured both to the user's personal preferences and to his mission focus.

As a consequence of the mission-flexible need, SOF soldiers tend to utilize state-of-the-art firearms, sometimes of types beyond the means of the regular soldiery. We mustn't take this latter point too far, however, for SOCOM forces work within the same budgetary and operational landscape as the wider military, which means in many cases SOF soldiers are equipped with just the same weaponry as regular troops. The M4A1 Carbine, for example, is as ubiquitous among SOF as it is among the broader US forces. In this study, therefore, we will focus on firearms that are either the province of SOF exclusively or principally, and on the accessories and options that can transform a regular firearm into something more tactically nuanced. Most of our analysis will focus on weapon types issued since the late 1990s. As we shall see, the last 30 years have witnessed some major leaps forward in military firearms, not so much in their fundamental operating principles (these largely remain the same as they were at the end of World War II), but in the realms of material construction, modularity, and sighting. The firearms used by the SOF community often represent the highest expressions of these technological advances, and as such represent a fascinating arsenal for our study.

DEVELOPMENT

Innovation and adaptation

HANDGUNS

In the late 1980s the US SOF community was still somewhat dependent upon vintage military semi-automatic handguns for their sidearms, specifically the .45 ACP Colt M1911 and occasionally the proven 9×19mm Browning GP-35 High Power, but they had also bought into the 9×19mm Beretta M9, which had taken over from the Colt M1911 as the standard US military pistol in 1985. There were, however, some more distinctive weapons in the SOF inventory, such as the 9×19mm Smith & Wesson Mk 22 Mod 0 "Hush Puppy" semi-automatic pistol, so named after one of its tactical purposes – silencing guard dogs. It was essentially a suppressed Smith & Wesson Model 39 fitted with a bulbous Mk 3 suppressor, plus a slide lock which, if engaged, prevented the slide from cycling following the shot, further reducing the noise signature. Using the "Hush Puppy" with subsonic Mk 144 158-grain green-tipped full metal jacket (FMJ) rounds reduced the noise of the pistol even further. It is not known (at least to the author) whether the "Hush Puppy" saw any combat use from 1980 onward, but it certainly remained in the SEALs' arsenal at least through to the end of the Cold War.

Revolvers

Another species of legacy weapons were revolvers. Although semi-automatic handguns offered numerous advantages over the revolver – higher magazine capacity (sometimes more than double), better recoil characteristics, faster reload, to name but three – what the revolver did offer, however, was better over-the-beach (OTB) reliability (although all modern SEAL handguns are designed with OTB rating in mind). OTB refers to the use of a firearm or piece of equipment during the movement

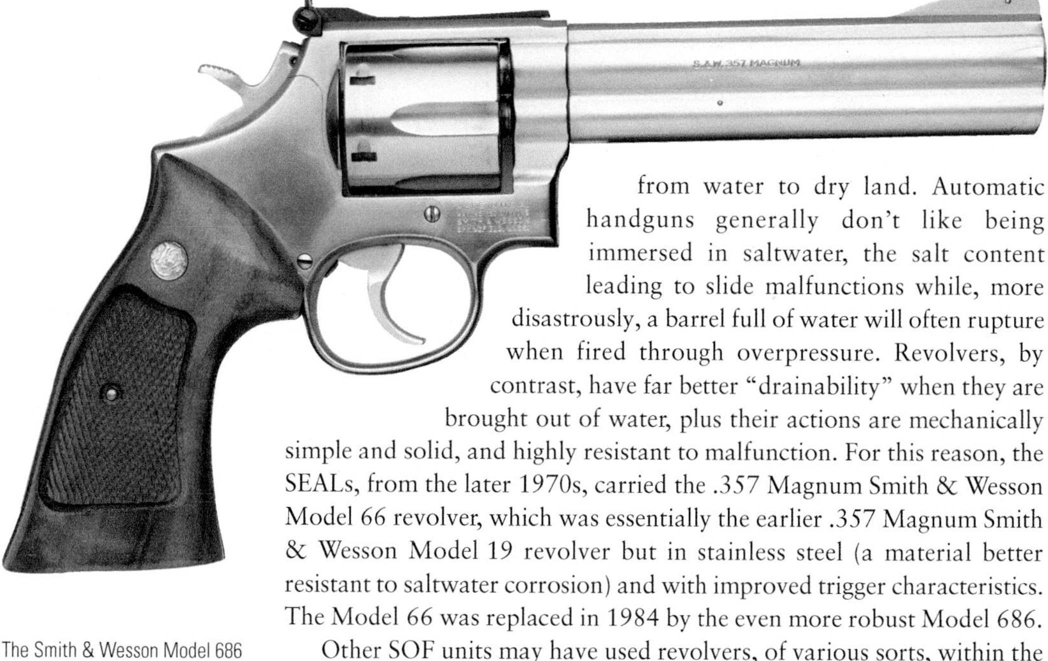

from water to dry land. Automatic handguns generally don't like being immersed in saltwater, the salt content leading to slide malfunctions while, more disastrously, a barrel full of water will often rupture when fired through overpressure. Revolvers, by contrast, have far better "drainability" when they are brought out of water, plus their actions are mechanically simple and solid, and highly resistant to malfunction. For this reason, the SEALs, from the later 1970s, carried the .357 Magnum Smith & Wesson Model 66 revolver, which was essentially the earlier .357 Magnum Smith & Wesson Model 19 revolver but in stainless steel (a material better resistant to saltwater corrosion) and with improved trigger characteristics. The Model 66 was replaced in 1984 by the even more robust Model 686.

The Smith & Wesson Model 686 was built with durability in mind, having a heavy and solid frame capable of handling repeated firing with the .357 loads. (© Royal Armouries PR.8699)

Other SOF units may have used revolvers, of various sorts, within the context of covert operations. (A small snub-nose .38 revolver, for example, offers the ultimate concealment.) Yet the inexorable movement toward semi-automatic handguns, which proliferated and diversified during the 1980s, meant that revolvers largely became a weapon of the past by the end of that decade. In the following section on handguns, therefore, we will examine the favored models of SOCOM semi-automatics from the late 1980s onward.

M1911 variants

The US military's love affair with the Colt M1911 pistol has been through its ups and downs since the 1980s, but the fondness for the .45 ACP cartridge wedded to the M1911 action has never entirely died out in the SOCOM community, particularly among the US Marine Corps' SOF elements. During the 1980s and 1990s, legacy stocks of M1911s remained in the hands of some Marine Corps SOF units and also in Delta Force, with unit armorers making adjustments and modifications to suit the operator's requirements. The replacement of internal parts, slides, and grip profiles was ultimately formalized in the mid-1980s in the M45 MEU(SOC) pistol – Marine Expeditionary Unit (Special Operations Capable). Essentially these weapons were rebuilt around an existing frame, and the resulting handguns mainly went to Force Recon, Marine Corps Special Operations Command, Detachment One (MCSOCOM Det-1), and Raider Battalions.

Demand for the M45 MEU(SOC) eventually outstripped supply, especially with the establishment of Marine Corps Forces Special Operations Command (MARSOC) in 2006, and so the Marine Corps turned to sourcing its M1911s from a commercial supplier (Kimber), and labeling them the Interim CQB Pistol. In 2010, the Marine Corps issued

A US Marine tries his hand with the .45 ACP M45 MEU(SOC) pistol, the M1911 heritage of the weapon clearly visible. The force of recoil from the handgun is apparent, this being one of the reasons why many military units opt for 9×19mm Parabellum handguns. (Lance Corporal Kamran Sadaghiani/Wikimedia/ Public Domain)

a requirement for a new off-the-shelf .45 ACP handgun to replace the M45 MEU(SOC) and ICQB Pistol. Various designs were submitted, but the one selected was a modified Colt O1980RG (Rail Gun) pistol, which was designated the M45A1 Close Quarter Battle Pistol (CQBP). With its stainless-steel finish, match-grade barrel, and under-frame rail, the M45A1 is a classic handgun repackaged for the modern era.

SIG Sauer handguns

SIG Sauer has long had a high reputation within the US military. Indeed, the P226 semi-automatic pistol was in the final two, alongside the Beretta 92FS, in the competition to replace the Colt M1911 as the standard US military pistol, only losing out to the Beretta on cost. Nevertheless, the fine shooting characteristics of the SIG Sauers and their robust build quality made an impression on the SOF community, which began to adopt SIG Sauer handguns in the late 1980s, partly in response to some function problems with the Beretta M9 (Neville 2015: 25). The SEALs in particular purchased the P226, which is still in service to this day.

The P226 operates along the same mechanical principles as the locked-breech short-recoil pistols developed much earlier in the 20th century by the great John Moses Browning, although locking in the P226 is performed by an enlarged breech section sliding into the ejection port aperture. The P226 has a double-action/single-action (DA/SA) function, and a decocking lever just in front of the slide stop on the left-hand side, allowing the user to cock the gun (placing a round in the chamber) but then decock the hammer for safe storage in a holster. Should the gun be required for action, all the user then has to do is draw it and pull the trigger in DA mode to fire. The P226 is available in four calibers, and the SEALs have made use of two of those (9mm Parabellum and .40 S&W). The P226 also evolved into the SOCOM-specific Mk 25 Mod 0, which is essentially the P226 with a Picatinny rail at the front of the lower frame, mainly intended for fitting tactical weapon lights and laser pointers. The Mk 25 also has an anti-corrosion coating on

ABOVE LEFT
A SIG Sauer P226. The latest versions of the handgun feature front cocking serrations on the slide, to give the user an additional point of purchase during loading, chamber inspections, and disassembly. (© Royal Armouries PR.2254)

ABOVE RIGHT
The SIG Sauer P228, known in US military use as the M11. The M11 is a 9mm-only weapon. Its standard magazine capacity is 13 rounds, but it can take the P226's 15- or 20-round magazines. (US Air Force/Wikimedia/Public Domain)

all internal parts (important for operators who might immerse their weapons in saltwater) and SIGLITE Night Sights. DEVGRU operators have also used the Mk 25 with an extended threaded barrel mounting an Advanced Armament Corp. (AAC) suppressor. Magazine capacity on the P226/Mk 25 can rise to 20 or even 30 rounds, with extended magazines.

The P226 was just the first of several SIG Sauer handguns that made their way into SOF arsenals. In 1989, the P228, a compact 9mm version of the P226 with a standard magazine capacity of 13 rounds, although longer 15- or 20-round P226 magazines can also be used, was adopted as the M11. The M11 was utilized by SOF operators who wanted a highly concealable handgun, but one that retained a decent magazine capacity. For those SEALs (principally the DEVGRU operators) requiring something even smaller, the 9mm SIG Sauer P239 was an option, this being a diminutive pistol with just eight rounds of ammunition in its single-stack magazine.

SIG Sauer handguns have been a niche corner of the US military market for 30 years, but recent events have changed the equation significantly. On January 19, 2017, it was announced that the SIG Sauer P320 had won the two-year XM17 Modular Handgun System (MHS) competition, the US Army and US Air Force competition for a new service handgun to replace the Beretta M9 and also the M11. As the name of the competition implies, the P320 is a modular weapon, capable of firing 9×19mm Parabellum, .357 SIG, .40 S&W, and .45 ACP through either a simple barrel change or the use of a caliber conversion kit. The polymer grip frames can be switched between four sizes of frames (full, carry, compact, and sub-compact) and three sizes of grips, to adjust to hand sizes and portability requirements. All of the frame assemblies bar the sub-compact feature a Picatinny rail at the front for tactical accessories. The P320's operating controls are fully ambidextrous and unlike the P226 it is a striker-fired pistol, which offers some advantages of mechanical simplicity over hammer-fired guns; by housing the firing mechanism within a self-contained stainless-steel fire-control unit, the structure of the handgun can be modified around the unit without having to change the firing mechanism.

In military service the P320 will be known as the M17 (full size) and M18 (carry). At the time of writing, the M17/M18 are in the early stages of entering US military service, the first examples having gone into service

A SIG Sauer P226 Mk 25 fitted with a SureFire X300 Ultra LED Weapon Light on its MIL-STD-1913 Picatinny-type rail rather than the more typical groove rail. Note the US Navy Silver Anchor on the weapon's slide. (DR8CO/Wikimedia/ CC BY-SA 4.0)

with the US Army's 101st Airborne Division in November 2017. The plan is for all US Army and US Marine Corps handguns to be replaced by the M17/M18 within a decade, and given the high qualities of the P320 it is likely that the weapon will become a SOF standard pistol as well.

Glock handguns

Glock handguns, first introduced with the Glock 17 in 1982, changed the face of pistol technology and design, with their combination of polymer frame, striker-fired mechanism, absence of manual safety, reliability, DA/SA mechanism, and ergonomic good sense. The Glock family is now extremely broad, catering for all manner of configuration and caliber requirements, and it has become literally the world's best-selling handgun, equipping armed forces, police forces, and millions of civilians globally.

Standard-issue Glocks have been used widely in SOCOM units, principally the SEALs, US Special Forces, and Rangers, but it was Delta Force that led the way with its acquisition of 9mm and .45 ACP Glocks in the 1990s. A variety of Glocks have made their way into SOF hands, but the

BELOW LEFT
A Gen 1 Glock 19. At the time of writing, the Glock handguns are at Gen 5 in their evolution, having adopted numerous improvements to their ergonomics and functionality. All SOCOM Glocks, for example, have accessory mounting rails cut into the front lower frame and changeable backstraps. (© Royal Armouries PR.8078)

BELOW RIGHT
A Gen 3 Glock 23 with .40 S&W ammunition. (Canon67/ Wikimedia/Public Domain)

most popular are essentially the best-selling Glock models, specifically the Glock 17 and 19 in 9×19mm and the Glock 22 and 23 in .40 S&W. (The Glock 19 and the Glock 23 are basically compact versions of the other weapons in their caliber.) Although off-the-shelf handguns are used, the Glocks in SOF hands have acquired the usual range of accessories, including weapon lights, red-dot sights, extended magazines, and suppressors.

Heckler & Koch handguns

In terms of handguns, Heckler & Koch has developed a particularly strong relationship with US naval SOF, designing weapons that are well-suited to the US Navy's exacting requirements. During the 1980s and 1990s, various Heckler & Koch models used by European SOF made their way into US SOCOM service.

The first of these seems to have been the P9S-N (Navy), of which the SEALs appear to have been the primary user. The P9S-N was a small 9×19mm handgun operating on a distinctive version of the roller-delayed blowback. This system meant that the barrel was fixed (rather than hinging), making it more convenient to fit a sound suppressor. The action was SA/DA, the P9S-N also featuring a decocking lever that could both decock the hammer and recock it again for a single-action shot. Portable and reliable, the P9S-N was a handy gun, albeit a little restricted by its nine-round magazine capacity.

A major conceptual step forward in SOCOM handgun design, described in more detail in the "Use" chapter below, was the Offensive Handgun Weapons System (OHWS) program – essentially the competition for a new SOF handgun with more offensive capabilities in the CQB role – that began in 1991. The outcome was the adoption, in 1996, of the Heckler & Koch Mk 23 Mod 0 short-recoil, SA/DA handgun with a mechanism based on the Browning action, the material construction being highly resistant to corrosion. The Mk 23 has some modern features appreciated by SOF, notably a decocking lever and ambidextrous safety and magazine release. The Mk 23 was a .45 ACP weapon (ten- or 12-round magazines), and was also robust enough to

A 9×19mm Heckler & Koch P9S handgun, here shown with its slide in the locked-back position. Extended threaded barrels are available to allow the fitting of a suppressor. (Rizuan/Wikimedia/ CC BY-SA 3.0)

THE GLOCK EXPOSED

9×19mm Gen 4 Glock 17

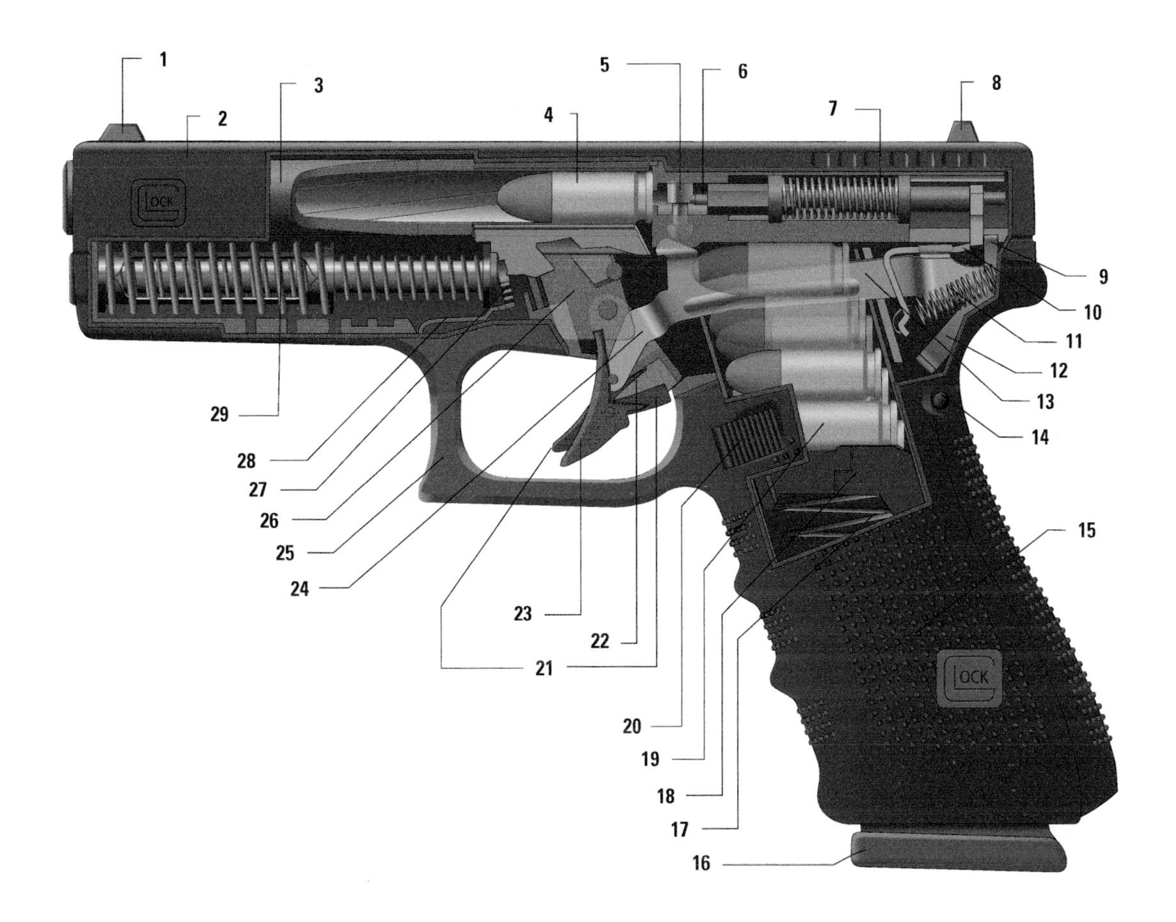

1. Front sight
2. Slide
3. Barrel
4. Cartridge in chamber
5. Firing pin safety and spring
6. Firing pin
7. Firing pin spring
8. Rear sight
9. Connector
10. Trigger bar cruciform kickup
11. Trigger spring
12. Connector
13. Trigger bar
14. Trigger housing pin
15. Textured pistol grip
16. Magazine floor plate
17. Magazine spring
18. Magazine follower
19. Cartridges in magazine
20. Magazine catch
21. Trigger safety
22. Trigger safety spring
23. Trigger
24. Trigger bar
25. Trigger guard
26. Locking block
27. Slide lock
28. Slide lock spring
29. Dual recoil spring assembly

A .45 ACP Heckler & Koch Mk 23 SOCOM pistol, fitted with a suppressor and with a tactical laser aiming module locked onto the rail groove on the front lower frame. The safety switch is ambidextrous, repeated on the other side of the weapon. (Joe Loong/Wikimedia/CC BY-SA 2.0)

take more powerful +P ammunition. To give the weapon its true offensive capability, however, it came with the ability to fit a laser aiming module (LAM) and a suppressor.

The Mk 23 appears good on paper, but reports suggest that it has not been popular in widespread front-line use, mainly on account of its weight and bulk – with a LAM and a Knight's Armament Company (KAC) suppressor fitted, it weighs a substantial 5lb. Yet the Mk 23 has been used successively and appreciatively by the SEALs and SEAL Delivery Teams (SDTs), who appreciate its resistance to saltwater immersion (the proprietary maritime finish has been laboratory tested in salt/fog spray chambers for up to 96 hours), general reliability (in Phase II trials, 6,027 mean rounds between failure; temperature parameters of -25°F to 140°F), and the impressive accuracy of the 6in barrel with polygonal rifling. The Mk 23 has succeeded in meeting the criteria of an "offensive handgun," albeit in the hands of a relative few specialists.

Another Heckler & Koch staple for SOCOM, mainly for DEVGRU, is the .45 ACP HK45C handgun. This emerged from the US Military Joint Combat Pistol (JCP) program to replace the standard Beretta M9 handgun, based on a specification for a .45 ACP handgun with an integrated Picatinny rail and the ability to take a suppressor. The JCP program petered out in 2006, but the Heckler & Koch contribution to the effort, the .45 ACP HK45 short-recoil handgun feeding from a ten-round magazine, aroused the interest of SOCOM units, especially the SEALs. Heckler & Koch invested heavily in the HK45's ergonomics, including an ambidextrous slide release, ergonomic grip, and changeable grip backstraps, to enable the weapon to be adjusted for different hand sizes. It was the more compact HK45C, however, that was officially adopted by the SEALs, in 2010, with the official title of Mk 24 Mod 0 Combat Assault Pistol. This weapon could take both LAM and suppressor, but it is designed for concealability, with a slimline grip profile, compressed dimensions, and smooth edges, so it can be hidden easily under clothing.

SUBMACHINE GUNS

In the first decade of SOCOM, the submachine gun (SMG) was still an important component of the SOF arsenal. The focus on counterterrorism operations that characterized the 1970s and 1980s gave high-quality SMGs, such as Heckler & Koch's defining 9×19mm MP5 series, a natural home within the SOF community. The SMG offered decisive and controllable full-automatic fire at close ranges (up to *c*.200m/219yd), in a weapon whose relatively compact dimensions made it convenient to use in CQB settings. The SMG also had limited penetration, which meant that it was practical for use in hostage-rescue missions where the shooters might have to avoid rounds passing through the enemy and into nearby hostages or bystanders.

During the 1980s, it was the MP5 that reigned supreme in SOCOM inventories. Firing from a closed bolt (meaning that the only mass shifting forward on firing was the firing pin), the MP5 was highly accurate, and could be fitted with various tactical accessories, such as flashlights and image intensifiers, although these were bulky affairs at the time and did little to improve handling qualities. Three versions of the MP5 became popular in SOCOM. The MP5-N was essentially the standard MP5, but with an ambidextrous trigger group, a rubber-padded retractable stock, and a threaded muzzle for fitting a suppressor. The MP5K-N was the Navy version of the *kurz* (short) variant, a cut-down version that, with the stock folded, could even be hidden away under a coat or in a small bag. A vertical foregrip was provided so the user could manage the increased rate of fire (900rd/min, as opposed to the 800rd/min of the standard MP5). The MP5K-N had the "Navy" trigger group and threaded muzzle. It also led in turn, in 1991, to the MP5K-PDW (Personal Defense Weapon), designed principally for SOF aircraft and vehicle crews. The MP5K-PDW included a side-folding Choate stock, a three-lug barrel for the quick-detachable Qual-A-Tec suppressor, and a three-round burst setting. The final MP5 variant used by SOCOM was the MP5SD-N, instantly recognizable through its

The Heckler & Koch MP5K is a compact variant within the MP5 family, and has been used by various SOCOM units for covert operations. With its stock folded the weapon measures just 14.5in. Its main shortcoming is the formidable muzzle blast produced when the weapon is fired. (US Air Force/Wikimedia/Public Domain)

With its stock collapsed, the MP7 measures just 16.3in. This particular weapon is fitted with the 20-round magazine, which sits flush with the bottom of the pistol grip, and also has an EOTech sight for quick target acquisition. (© Royal Armouries PR.13964)

integral (although detachable) aluminum sound suppressor. The suppressor was effective, with the tradeoff that it reduced the muzzle velocity of rounds to subsonic levels, although this was part and parcel of the overall sound reduction.

The MP5 and its ilk were, and remain, fine weapons; yet during the 1980s and emphatically so in the 1990s, US and indeed global SOF began to move away from SMGs in favor of carbines. Carbines offered virtually the same dimensions as SMGs, but with the ballistic superiority of firing the 5.56×45mm rifle round. This not only meant that the operator could achieve better results when firing through material obstructions or body armor, but he could also switch from close-in engagements measured in mere meters through to medium-distance engagements out to 275m (301yd). Thus SMGs have been massively sidelined in favor of their carbine relatives, including within SOCOM.

There is some life in the SMG story yet, however. The MP5 remains in SEAL arsenals, indeed the MP5SD-N has proven its continuing utility even in Iraq and Afghanistan, where operators have appreciated its silent qualities during covert direct-action missions. Another more modern acquisition has been small numbers of the Heckler & Koch MP7A1. This gas-operated weapon straddles the SMG and carbine categories (it is actually classified as a PDW) and features a rotating bolt with a 950rd/min rate of fire, top and side rails and a collapsible stock, folding front grip, and a magazine well in the pistol grip. The MP7A1 is so well balanced around the grip that it can be fired one-handed. Most significant, however, is the weapon's 4.6×30mm ammunition, with low recoil characteristics but excellent penetration on account of the bullet's hardened-steel penetrator. The MP7A1 has mainly been used by DEVGRU, but its ammunition choice divides opinion and its adoption has been limited.

CARBINES AND ASSAULT RIFLES

It is in the world of carbines and assault rifles that SOCOM troops have witnessed some of the more significant degrees of change since the 1990s. There are four main factors that have governed developments in this field. The first is modularity – assault rifles have acquired a degree of modularity, i.e. a configuration that allows the user to change key components and thereby modify the weapon to meet the specific requirements of the mission. The second is ergonomics – the weapon furniture should be designed to allow some measure of personalized fit, such as stocks that can be extended or collapsed to accommodate length of pull (the distance from the rear of the stock to the trigger), or rail fittings that permit the flexible fitting of foregrips. The third relates to accessories – most modern assault rifles now come with rails mounted on the forend and the top of the receiver, enabling the fitting of multiple tactical accessories, including tactical flashlights, LAMs, combat optics of numerous varieties, thermal imagers, and underbarrel grenade launchers. The application of these accessories can radically alter the combat capability of the weapon. The last of the four is caliber – what is the right battlefield caliber is a debate that began in the 1960s and continues to rage today. Suffice to say that while 5.56×45mm NATO has dominated with SOCOM assault rifles, there are now signs of movement in different directions, explored below.

The AR-15 platform

The AR-15 platform, as expressed in the M16 series of rifles and the M4 series of carbines, is by far the most prevalent of the assault-rifle types in SOCOM service, as indeed it is in the wider US military. By the time of SOCOM's formation in April 1987, the now standard M16A2 was already in use with US SOF. Yet an important legacy of the Vietnam era was the development of a carbine version, variously known as the CAR-15, Colt Commando, XM177E2 (type classification), and GAU/5A (in US Air Force SOF). The Commando featured an 11.5in barrel (originally just 10in, but later lengthened based on field feedback) with an oversized flash hider to help cope with the heavy muzzle flash, plus an extendable stock and a redesigned cylindrical forend. The platform proved popular with SOF, and the utility of the carbine format in general led to the development of the M4 series from the mid-1980s (although official adoption of the M4 did not come until 1994), which eventually settled on a 14.5in barrel.

Emerging during the 1960s, the XM177 was a leading example of the US military's progressive shift toward carbine firepower, which came to fruition in the later widespread adoption of the M4 Carbine, including among US SOF. (© Royal Armouries PR.5380)

The SOPMOD Block I accessory kit, as described in an official poster. Note how much of the accessorization is given to various sight options. (US DoD/Wikimedia/Public Domain)

SOCOM operators have utilized all standard-issue variants of the M16 and M4, especially the M4A1, the latter offering the utility of a full-length Picatinny rail across the top of the receiver and around all compass points of the forend, allowing for all manner of accessorization. The M4A1 also featured a heavier barrel, called the SOCOM Profile barrel, which allowed the weapon to deliver more rapid and intensive full-auto fire with a reduced risk of barrel distortion and "cook-offs."

Being standard-issue firearms, there have also been some AR-15 variants specific to SOCOM forces. The SEALs, for example, adopted the M16A3 in limited numbers; the only difference in this model from the M16A2 was that it replaced the three-round burst setting with a full-automatic capability. It is the M4A1, however, that has received the greatest degree of use by SOCOM, the carbine being the most practical version for many of the SOF roles.

The critical SOF optimization of the M4 platform has been the result of the implementation of Special Operations Peculiar Modification (SOPMOD) kits. The SOPMOD kit, introduced in "Block I" by the end of the 1990s, is an approved package of accessory items, which the operator can configure according to operational requirements. The Block I kit featured:

- 4× Day Optical Scope (Trijicon TA01NSN 4×32mm Advanced Combat Optical Gunsight – ACOG)

- Reflex Sight (Trijicon Model RX01M4A1)
- ECOS-N Optical Sight (red-dot-type reflex sight, a variant of the Aimpoint CompM2)
- Rail Interface System (MIL-STD-1913)
- Vertical Forward Handgrip
- Quick-attach/-detach M203 grenade launcher mount and sight
- M203 40mm Barrel Assembly
- Sound Suppressor Kit (KAC quick-detach sound suppressor – QDSS)
- AN/PEQ-2 Infrared Illuminator (Insight Technology)
- AN/PEQ-5 Carbine Visible Laser (Insight Technology)
- AN/PVS-17A Mini Night Vision Sight (Insight Technology)
- AN/PSQ-18A M203 Day/Night Sight (Insight Technology)
- Visible Bright Light (Insight Technology Visible Light Illuminator – VLI)
- Universal Pocket Scope Mount
- Combat Sling
- Sloping Cheek Weld Buttstock (referred to as the "Crane Stock")

This extensive kit had a transformative effect on the basic M4 carbine. A typical setup might be the ACOG for day ops, or for night missions the AN/PVS-17A and AN/PEQ-5 plus VLI. Whatever the configuration, the SOPMOD elements were there to "increase operator survivability and lethality by enhanced weapon performance, target acquisition, signature suppression, and fire control" (Taylor 2005: 4).

Following SOPMOD Block I, there were a series of incremental phased replacements and modifications, specifically:

- M4A1 RIS II (Rail Interface System) and RIS II FSP (Front Sight Post) full-length handguards (Daniel Defense)
- SU-223/PVS Tactical Illuminator Flashlight (Insight Technology M3X)
- SU-238/PVS Tactical Laser Illuminator (Insight Technology M6X)
- SU-231/PEQ HOLOgraphic Weapon Sight (EOTech 553)
- SU-237/PVS Sight Unit (Trijicon ACOG TA01 ECOS 4× Scope)
- AN/PVS-17 Product Improvement Kit
- BUIS II

From 2005, SOPMOD Block II items gradually came into issue, although the Block I element would continue in service and distribution. Block II included a range of improved optics, both for day and night use, additional rail systems for different lengths of barrel, and some upgraded gun lights.

The SOPMOD kits have been adopted throughout the US SOF community, and have transformed the basic M4A1 into a versatile weapon

A US Army Special Forces soldier from the 10th Special Forces Group conducts training with a CQBR carbine. The weapon is fitted with a Daniel Defense RIS II Rail Interface System and SOPMOD Block II accessories. (Defense Dept photo by Staff Sgt Michael R. Noggle)

ABOVE LEFT
This DEVGRU (SEAL Team Six) operator is performing close-protection duties in Afghanistan. He is armed with a Mk 18 Mod 0 CQBR carbine, fitted with a red-dot sight and a tactical foregrip. (US DoD)

ABOVE RIGHT
A Navy SEAL trains his Mk 18 Mod 0 carbine, fitted with a Knight's Armament Company (KAC) suppressor, SureFire tactical light, and an Aimpoint red-dot sight. The Mk 18 is often used in ship-boarding operations. (US Navy photo by Mass Communication Specialist 2d Class Martin L. Carey)

system. At the time of writing, there are sketchy discussions about a Block III package. Furthermore, upgraded types of optics and other accessories regularly enter the system and appear on service weapons, depending on issues such as budget availability and distribution.

Although the M4A1 in its standard 14.5in barrel configuration is a short weapon in itself, the SEALs' requirement for an even more compact weapon, principally for shipboard operations and hostage rescue, led to the development of the Close Quarter Battle Receiver (CQBR). The CQBR is a replacement upper receiver fitted with a 10.3in barrel, reducing the overall length of the weapon to 30in with the stock extended, as opposed to 33in for the standard M4A1. The assembled weapon is type classified as the Mk 18 CQBR, and like its longer relatives it can be fitted with the SOPMOD accessories; a favored setup with the SEALs is the ECOS-N optical sight plus the KAC QDSS-NT4 Suppressor.

The Mk 16 Mod 0 SCAR-L

The Mk 16 Mod 0 SCAR-L is a new generation of 5.56×45mm carbine developed by Fabrique Nationale of Belgium. "SCAR" actually refers to a family of weapons, not a single firearm, the abbreviation standing for "Special Operations Forces Combat Assault Rifles." The firearms were developed in response to a 2004 SOCOM solicitation for a carbine family that used both 5.56mm and 7.62mm rounds but shared commonality in many components, ergonomics, etc. The family also had to demonstrate full modularity, including switching upper receivers, barrels of different lengths, and a new grenade-launching module.

The Mk 16 Mod 0 (the FN SCAR-L; L for "Light") is the 5.56mm member of the family. Instantly recognizable by its chunky profile and hinged folding stock, the SCAR has a two-receiver design – the lower receiver is made from polymer and the upper receiver from a single piece of aluminum, with rails across the top of the receiver (full length), down the sides, and underneath the forend, although the side rails can be removed. The rifle is gas operated with a short-stroke gas piston, meaning

The 5.56×45mm FN SCAR-L, here with the short 10in CQC barrel plus the 40mm FN40GL Mk 2 grenade launcher fitted as an underbarrel option; note how both triggers can be pulled without changing the hand position. (© Royal Armouries XXX.288)

that it avoids some of the heat build-up issues associated with the direct-impingement gas system of the AR-15 platform. To satisfy the modularity requirements, Fabrique Nationale gave the SCAR three different barrel-length options: while the Mk 16 CQC (Close Quarters Combat) had a 10in barrel, the Mk 16 STD (Standard) had a 14in barrel and the Mk 16 LB (Long Barrel) had an 18in barrel. The SCAR could also take the Enhanced Grenade Launching Module (EGLM), or Mk 13 Mod 0, a 40mm grenade launcher that can either be fired mounted onto the weapon or as a standalone device.

SOCOM combat trials of the SCAR began in 2009 with the US Army Rangers, and the Mk 16 Mod 0 subsequently went into service with the Navy SEALs, Air Force Special Tactics, and in small numbers among the Army Special Forces Operational Detachments Alpha (ODAs) serving in Afghanistan. Yet the Mk 16's procurement history has been complex. Having been acquired by several SOF units, it was then canceled from the SOCOM procurement program in 2010, SOCOM stating: "The Mk 16 does not provide enough of a performance enhancement over the M4 to justify spending limited USSOCOM funds when competing priorities are taken into consideration" (quoted in Crane 2011). Nevertheless, the Mk 16 seemed to find particular popularity with the SEALs (less so with the Rangers), and in 2011 the SEALs placed additional orders for the weapon, which serves on with the force today.

The HK416

Like the SCAR, the Heckler & Koch HK416 is another weapon spawned from collaboration between US SOF and a major European arms manufacturer. The program that led to the weapon was SOCOM's Confined Spaces Carbine in the late 1990s, which issued a requirement for a highly compact weapon for use in JSOC tactical units (Neville 2015: 124–25). Delta Force collaborated directly with Heckler & Koch in the development, and the result was the HK416, which entered service with Delta Force in 2004, replacing its M4s.

Again like the SCAR, the HK416 moved away from the direct-impingement gas system of the AR-15 platform in favor of the short-stroke

THE HK416 EXPOSED

5.56×45mm HK416

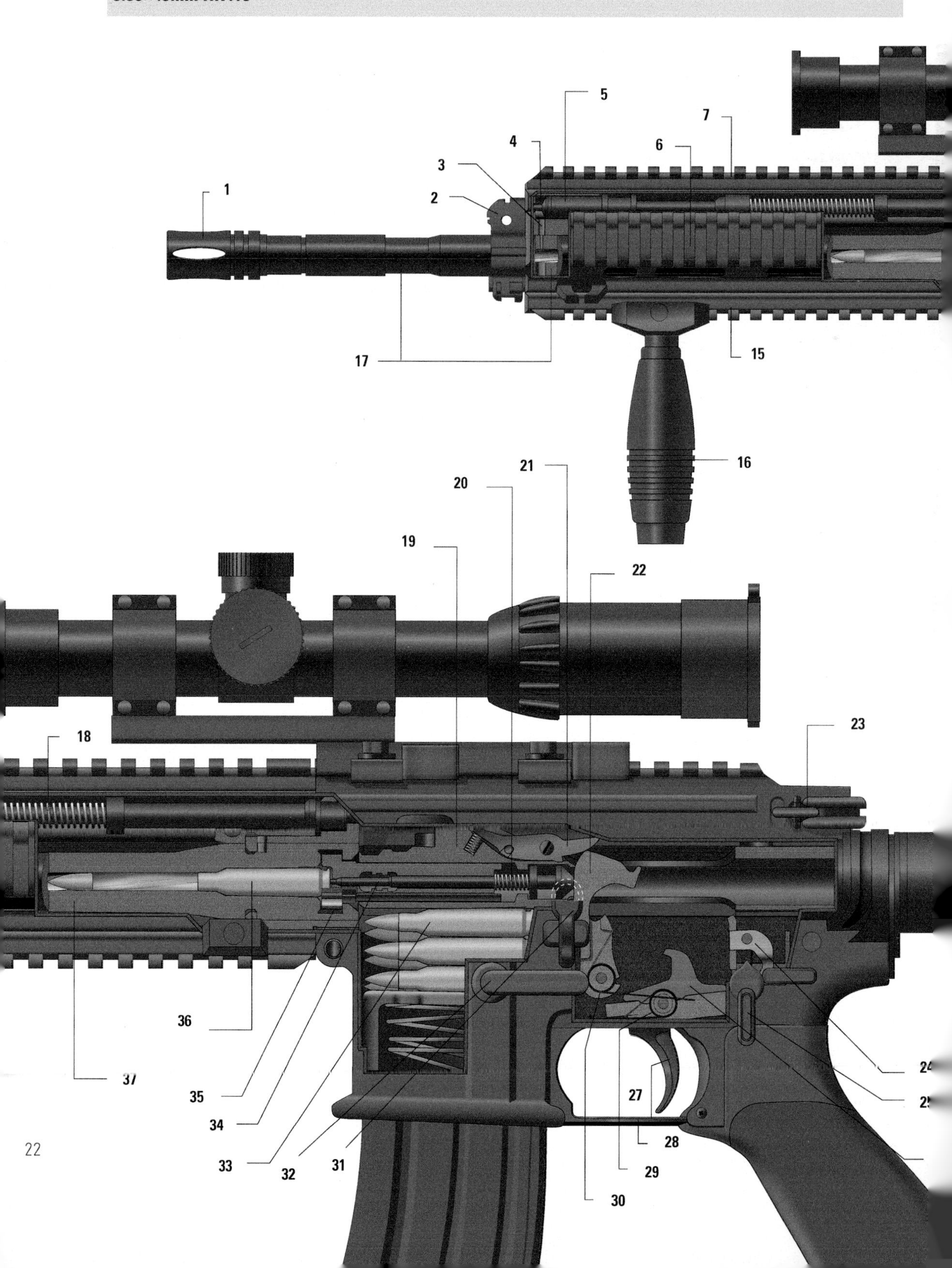

1. Compensator
2. Gas block
3. Gas vent
4. Gas cylinder
5. Piston head
6. Side rail
7. Upper rail
8. Telescopic sight
9. Buffer
10. Recoil spring
11. Butt
12. Butt plate
13. Pistol grip
14. Magazine spring
15. Lower rail
16. Forward grip
17. Barrel
18. Piston spring
19. Bolt carrier
20. Firing pin spring
21. Firing pin catch
22. Hammer
23. Charger handle assembly
24. Sear automatic assembly
25. Selector switch
26. Disconnector
27. Trigger
28. Trigger guard
29. Trigger spring
30. Hammer spring
31. Bolt catch
32. Magazine catch
33. Cartridges in magazine
34. Firing pin
35. Bolt
36. Cartridge in chamber
37. Barrel (cutaway)

gas piston, this system derived from that used on Heckler & Koch's globally successful G36 assault rifle. (Tests showed that an unsuppressed HK416 had only about 10 percent of the carbon build-up compared to that of an M4A1.) The furniture permits a typically high degree of accessorization; there are MIL-STD-1913 rails on all four sides of the forearm, and the rail forearm is also of the free-floating type, meaning that it does not touch the hammer-forged barrel, and thus makes the weapon more accurate. Multiple lengths of barrel are available, from 9in up to 20in, although the most common barrels in DEVGRU use are the 10.5in and the 14.5in, variously fitted with suppressors. Feed is from ten-, 20-, or 30-round detachable box magazines, although DEVGRU operators have been known to fit their weapons with SureFire 60-round magazines. If there are any concerns that such large-capacity magazines might encourage barrel-wearing fire, the HK416's barrel has been developed to offer a 20,000-round service life. Further contributions to reliability come from OTB modifications; there are drainage holes in the bolt carrier and buffer system. There is a six-position telescopic stock, so that the user can adjust the weapon's length of pull, and there is also a small storage space in the stock for holding items such as spare weapon-sight batteries.

The HK416, through a combination of accuracy and impressive reliability, has spread through SOCOM, but with principal concentrations in Delta Force and DEVGRU. The weapon's greatest claim to fame is undoubtedly that it is the rifle that was used to kill Osama bin Laden during the SEAL Team Six raid on his compound on May 2, 2011.

The SIG Sauer MCX, "Rattler," and SURG

Bringing the SOCOM carbine story up to date are the efforts of German company SIG Sauer, which we have already met in the context of handgun development. Introduced in 2015, the SIG Sauer MCX is another short-stroke piston gas-operated weapon, with a folding stock, rail mountings, and offering selective fire from 30-round box magazines. That much is familiar, but where this weapon excels is in its ability both to swap the barrel length – options are 9in for CQB work or 16in as a standard combat carbine – and also calibers. The caliber change is performed through a quick-change barrel function; the barrel can be swapped out in a minute or so with basic tools. Although a caliber-change option is 7.62×39mm, the two cartridges preferred by SOCOM are the obvious 5.56×45mm and also the .300 AAC Blackout, the latter a 7.62×35mm round that delivers performance similar to that of the standard AK assault-rifle round, thus closing the gap between US weapons and the typical firepower encountered in places such as Afghanistan and the Middle East.

The core MCX has been developed into a handful of variants that have been drawn into various corners of the SOCOM arsenal. These include the MCX Low Visibility Assault Weapon (LVAW), which has an integral suppressor that takes the audible signature of the firearm down to a low-key "snap" (especially when used in conjunction with subsonic ammunition), the sound of the oscillating bolt rivaling that of the report at the muzzle. There is also a PDW version, the MCX "Rattler," which has a barrel length

The SIG Sauer MCX rifle entered SOCOM service in 2015, in limited numbers. The version seen here has the full-length 16in barrel, but the Short-Barreled Rifle (SBR) version has a barrel measuring just 9in. (Mike Searson/Wikimedia/CC BY-SA 4.0)

of just 5.5in, the carbine having an overall length of just 16in when the stock is in the folded position. As of late 2018, the MCX "Rattler" is only provided in .300 Blackout, making it an attractive combination of compactness and firepower for SOCOM users on covert operations.

Another SIG Sauer development at the time of writing is the recent SOCOM announcement that the German company has been selected to provide the Suppressed Upper Receiver Group (SURG). As the name suggests, this is not a complete weapon, but rather an upper receiver with detachable suppressor that can be fitted to the lower receiver of an M4. The kit also comes with a SIG Sauer folding stock for the M4A1. Reports indicate that one of the great strengths of the SURG is the effectiveness of the suppressor system – at the shooter's ear, the sound of the gunshot does not exceed 140dB. The SURG has also been constructed with maximum reliability for its demanding customer; the receiver has a service life of some 15,000–20,000 rounds, and during tests the SURG fired 1,200 rounds without any lubrication.

BATTLE AND DM RIFLES

The experience of US military combat in Afghanistan led to some hard questions being asked about caliber choice, in particular the suitability of the standard 5.56×45mm NATO round for combat ranges over about 475m (520yd). This has led in many cases to a drift back to the 7.62×51mm NATO round among SOF teams operating in open or mountainous terrain. Not only does the 7.62×51mm NATO round offer the ability to take shots up to and in excess of 730m (798yd), but it also can provide better penetrative effect at range against cover and body armor.

To be fair, this lesson about caliber actually predates the "War on Terror" from 2001. During the 1980s, the classic mix of firepower in a SOF team was the 5.56mm M4/M16 alongside soldiers armed with the venerable 7.62×51mm NATO M14 rifle, which had its ancestry back in the M1 Garand rifle. The M14 fulfilled what became known as the Designated Marksman (DM) or Squad Designated Marksman (SDM) role. The DM is an individual armed with an accurized rifle, fitted with advanced combat optics, who in combination with his weapon is able to take precision shots out through the 275–550m (301–601yd) range. A full-fledged sniper, in addition to his advanced field craft (actually one of the distinguishing elements of a sniper), is expert enough to shoot beyond the 550m (601yd) range, even up to and beyond 1,000m (1,094yd). In US service, DM rifles come in both 5.56mm and 7.62mm, the former accurized via heavier match-grade and free-floating barrels and sometimes superior ammunition; pure sniper rifles will rarely use 5.56mm, preferring instead heavier calibers such as .300 Winchester Magnum or .338 Lapua.

The proof of the DM concept, and the combat experience gained by SOCOM units over the last 40 years, has resulted in a range of fresh battle/DM rifle types on the SOF battlefield. Combined with the considerable interest in new cartridge types, the result is a body of arms that can now meet the enemy on equal terms across a far wider spectrum of combat ranges.

M14

The M14 has been a core battle rifle for the US military from its in-service introduction in 1959 through to the present day, despite its replacement as a standard-issue rifle in the US Army and Marine Corps from the mid-1960s. Firing the 7.62×51mm NATO round, it has been kept relevant through numerous modifications to its material build (such as folding stocks, integral bipods, and heavier barrels), the fitting of ever-more advanced day and night optics, and the use of precision ammunition, resulting not only in DM-capable models but also full semi-automatic sniper rifles such as the M21 and M25.

In its basic historical profile, the M14 is a gas-operated rifle with a 22in barrel and feeding from a 20-round box magazine. With good optics fitted, it can command range of more than 800m (875yd). Early SOCOM users of the M14 were Delta Force and the SEALs, who often customized their rifles with bespoke stocks, foregrips, and sight fittings. During the 1993 action in Mogadishu, for example, some of the Delta Force operators were armed with M14s. Historian of Special Forces firearms Leigh Neville notes that during the early 2000s Delta Force armorers made heavy modifications to the M14s then in service, cutting the barrels right back and replacing the stocks with lighter folding versions, to produce an M14 better suited to the portability requirements of SOF (Neville 2015: 165).

A more sophisticated evolution of the M14 is the Mk 14 Mod 0 Enhanced Battle Rifle (EBR), a pure DM weapon developed specifically to meet a request from the Navy SEALs in the early 2000s for a more compact M14 rifle, better suited to mobile ops. A variety of commercial and SOCOM organizations worked together to produce the Mk 14 Mod 0, which had an 18in barrel, a pistol grip, a lightweight aircraft-alloy chassis system stock (adjustable for length of pull and drop), a Harris bipod, four Picatinny rails around the forend, an improved flash hider, and the ability to mount a suppressor. Optics included models such as the Leupold Mk 4, M68 Close Combat Optic, and Nightforce NXS.

Mk 14 Mod 0 rifles have been, and remain, popular weapons within SOCOM, not only used by the Navy SEALs but also by MARSOC, Army SF ODAs, and Air Force Special Tactics units. The Mod 1 and Mod 2 variants have responded to requirements for changes, the Mod 1 having different furniture and a SureFire 762K-DE suppressor, while the Mod 2 had the more dramatic change of a 22in barrel, turning the weapon into more of a sniper tool.

SEAL Recon/Mk 12 Mod 0/1 SPR

During the 1990s there began explorations of ways in which the standard M4A1 Carbine could be modified to provide improved range, and better accuracy over that range. In essence, the effort was an attempt to create a weapon that occupied the midpoint between a full-length M16A2 and the carbine version. SEAL armorers, in the early part of the 1990s, improvised the necessary modifications, fitting the M4A1 with a 16in stainless-steel barrel and mounting a range of Leupold, Trijicon, and Nightforce optics, plus a folding stock. In performance the "Recon" or "Recce" rifle, as it was known, certainly improved on the range of the M4A1; it could take shots out to 400m (437yd) comfortably. It gained enough credibility to be produced in limited numbers by the Naval Surface Warfare Center, Crane Division, which introduced innovations such as a free-floating handguard, but complaints about the weapon's reliability, primarily in full-automatic mode, ensured that it would not be widely issued.

The Recon rifle, however, led to an official SOCOM requirement for just such a weapon, and in response Crane Division produced the Mk 12 Mod 0 Special Purpose Rifle (SPR), which went into service in 2002. (SPR originally stood for "Special Purpose Receiver," as it was originally intended as just a replacement upper, but it quickly evolved into a complete weapon.)

The SPR is a sophisticated 5.56mm weapon, at the heart of which is an 18in threaded-muzzle match-grade free-floating stainless-steel heavy barrel, with a 1:7 rifling twist ratio for the special Mk 262 Open Tip Match round (the SPR is not designed for standard-issue infantry ammunition). The configuration of the weapon is replete with all the rails, adjustable furniture and suppressor options you would expect, and a wide variety of optics are seen atop the receiver, giving the rifle a range of up to 800m (875yd).

The Mk 12 Mod 0, and its successor the Mk 12 Mod 1, have seen substantial service in the War on Terror, including in the hands of SEALs (especially DEVGRU), the US Army Rangers, and US Army Special Forces. Neville notes, however, that it has acquired many competitors, including the Mk 16 and Mk 17 SCAR, the HK416, and the SR-25 (Neville 2015: 163).

An SOF operator looks through the scope of a Mk 12 Mod 1 during training, September 2007. (US Navy photo by Mass Communication Specialist 2nd Class Eli J. Medellin/ Wikimedia/Public Domain)

A US Coast Guard Maritime Security Response Team Precision Marksmen Observer Team undergo range practice with SR-25 rifles. One of the virtues of the SR-25's semi-automatic system is that the shooter doesn't have to break hold following each shot to operate a bolt handle. (US Coast Guard photo by Petty Officer 2d Class Michael Anderson)

The SR-25/Mk 11 Mod 0/1

By 1990 that great name in modern modular firearms design, Eugene Stoner, was working for KAC, a firm with a deep-rooted history of supplying weaponry and parts for SOCOM firearms. Stoner was focusing on developing his 7.62×51mm AR-10 platform into something more commercially and militarily compelling. The result was the SR-25, which is a gas-operated, semi-automatic DM/sniper rifle with a free-floating 24in match-grade barrel, a fiberglass handguard, a MIL-STD-1913 rail atop the flat receiver, and a two-stage match-grade trigger. Despite being a semi-automatic system, fed from a 20-round box magazine, the SR-25 delivered 1 minute of angle (MOA) standard of accuracy.

During the early 1990s, and especially following the First Gulf War (1990–91), SOCOM units began to take notice of the SR-25, mainly on account of its excellent accuracy combined with its semi-automatic operating system, which meant that follow-up shots could be taken rapidly against multiple targets. The weapons principally went to Delta Force and the SEALs, where they were extensively field modified to meet operational requirements. In May 2000, however, Crane Division began producing an official SOCOM version, designated the Mk 11 Mod 0. This weapon had a shorter 20in barrel, a quick-detachable sound suppressor mount, a free-floating handguard rail system, and an M16A2 stock and pistol grip. Flip-up backup iron sights (BUIS) ensured that the Mk 11 Mod 0 could transition to CQB if required; the standard optic was the Leupold Mk 4 Mil-dot riflescope. Delta Force also produced a shorter version of the SR-25, known as the SR-25K, specifically for transitioning between long-range shooting and CQB; barrel lengths of 14.5in and 16in have been produced.

An M110 SASS rifle fitted with an AN/PVS-10 Sniper Night Sight (SNS). The sight is a day/night model, using a direct-view system for day use and third-generation image intensification for night use. (Photo Courtesy of PEO Soldier/Wikimedia/Public Domain)

The M110 SASS

Another DM weapon in use with SOCOM, principally with US Army Rangers and Special Forces, is the M110 Semi Automatic Sniper System (SASS). In the mid-2000s, having seen the SOCOM SR-25s in action, the wider US Army established a competition for a new semi-automatic DM rifle, a competition that KAC won with the M110. This rifle had a noticeable family connection with the SR-25/Mk 11 Mod 0, but featured a URX modular rail system with an integral folding front 600m (656yd) backup iron sight, a fixed but adjustable buttstock, and a flash hider on the barrel. The M110 SASS, with its 20in barrel, has experienced the same evolution toward shorter dimensions as the other weapons, with the US Army beginning the hunt for a shorter Compact Semi-Automatic Sniper System (CSASS) in 2012, as an actual replacement for the full-length M110. After a complex period of political maneuvering, in 2016 the US Army announced that Heckler & Koch would deliver the CSASS, in the form of the G28 semi-automatic rifle (a militarized version of the MR308 competition gun, and within the HK417 family), which in US service would be called the M110A1 CSASS. The M110A1 CSASS entered service with the US Marine Corps in 2018, and it remains to be seen how widespread it becomes in the SOCOM community.

This Navy SEAL aims his M110 SASS from a helicopter, August 2011. (United States Navy SEALs/Wikimedia/Public Domain)

A Heckler & Koch HK417 on display at a military fair in 2016. This appears to be the version with the full 20in barrel, which combined with the stability of the bipod would make is suited to sniping work up to 1,000m (1,094yd). (Rizuan/Wikimedia/ CC BY-SA 4.0)

The HK417

In service since 2005, the Heckler & Koch HK417 is essentially the 7.62×51mm model of the HK416 described above. The HK417 has mainly gone into the hands of DEVGRU and US Army Special Forces (it was rejected by Delta Force), and has been produced in three different barrel lengths in the standard model, each model having its own evocative name: the HK417 Assaulter, with 12in standard barrel; the HK417 Recce, with 16in standard or accurized barrel; and the HK417 Sniper, with 20in accurized barrel. The subsequent HK417A2 version, released in 2013, similarly categorized the weapons according to barrel length: 13in, 16.5in, and 20in.

The Mk 17 SCAR-H

The Mk 17 SCAR-H ("H" stands for "Heavy"), in operating system and layout, is essentially the aforementioned SCAR-L, but in 7.62×51mm caliber and three different barrel lengths: 13in, 16in, and 20in. The HK417 has in turn yielded the Mk 20 Mod 0 Sniper Support Rifle (SSR), based on the SCAR-H, which has an extended receiver rail to take a multiplicity of optics, an enhanced trigger, improvements to the barrel, plus a full adjustable but non-folding stock. Firing from its integral bipod, the SSR is capable, according to manufacturer claims, of sub-MOA accuracy out to and beyond 914m (1,000yd).

The relationship of the Mk 17 to SOCOM has been a complex one. Although SOCOM decided in 2010 to cancel Mk 16 acquisition (see above), it continued its commitment to the Mk 17, principally for reasons of budgetary efficiency, although many SOF units, and especially the US Army Rangers and US Navy SEALs, appreciated the Mk 17 tactically for its additional reach and penetration. Recognizing the need for a

This is the standard FN SCAR-H, fitted with a 16in barrel. Swapping the barrel out for a shorter CQB variant has been made simplicity itself; the whole process can be performed in roughly five minutes. (© Royal Armouries XXX.287)

5.56mm option, SOCOM authorized the development of a 5.56mm conversion kit for the Mk 17, which began to be fielded in 2011. Thus looking across SOCOM forces, we see 5.56mm and 7.62mm Mk 17s plus 5.56mm Mk 16s specifically with the SEALs.

SNIPER RIFLES

When SOCOM came into being in April 1987, the sniper rifles of the US SOF community were largely the same as those used in the regular military forces. These were divided into bolt-action types such as the US Army's M24 Sniper Weapon System (SWS) and the US Marine Corps' M40, both based on the Remington 700 rifle and chambered for 7.62×51mm caliber, and semi-automatic rifles such as the accurized M14s outlined above. The bolt-action types have not disappeared from the scene, despite their longevity; in updated form they have been used extensively in US deployments in Iraq and Afghanistan, the modern rifles featuring heavily redesigned furniture and chamberings for what have become more popular sniping calibers, such as .338 Lapua and .300 Winchester Magnum. As SOCOM requirements grew more focused during the 1990s and 2000s, however, the sniper rifles acquired more advanced ergonomics plus optics offering enhancements in clarity (day and night), tactical adjustment (in terms of reticle design and drop/windage adjustment), and improvements in resilience, supplemented by the growing use of laser rangefinding technologies.

One of the biggest areas of development in military sniper rifles of the last 30 years has actually been in cartridge and bullet design. The principal calibers of modern sniping rifles are 7.62×51mm and .308 Winchester (these are the most readily available on the commercial market), plus the aforementioned .338 Lapua and .300 Winchester Magnum, while for genuine anti-materiel purposes there is the .50-caliber BMG. Within each cartridge type, there have been refinements and innovations in bullet design, propellant loads, and other factors, all too complex to summarize here but all seeking to extend the effective range of the rifle, often well past the 1,000m (1,094yd) mark, while also making the bullet flight more resistant to interference from wind. Taken together with the excellence of US SOF sniper training, the combination of perfectionism in both rifle and cartridge design means that at ranges of under 1,500m (1,640yd) all enemies of the United States run the potential risk of sudden death from a single round.

.50-caliber rifles

SOCOM bought into the .50-caliber anti-materiel rifle from its earliest days. During the 1980s, US Army Special Forces acquired some early examples of the Barrett M82A1 rifle, a revolutionary recoil-operated semi-automatic weapon with a range in excess of 2,000m (2,188yd), feeding from a ten-round box magazine. The M82A1 would progressively embed itself in US military thinking, and in 2002 it was officially adopted as the M107 Special Application Scoped Rifle (SASR), later rebranded the Long Range Sniper Rifle (LRSR).

Two SEAL snipers in training. The man on the left is armed with a .50-caliber Mk 15 Mod 0 anti-materiel rifle (left) and his colleague has a 7.62mm Mk 11 Mod 0 semi-automatic sniper rifle (right). (US DoD)

Alongside Barrett, the McMillan company was another early provider of .50-caliber sniper rifles to SOCOM. The first McMillan .50-caliber rifle to be adopted by SOCOM troops (specifically the Navy SEALs) was the M88, a bolt-action weapon launching a 700-grain bullet, and SEAL teams took advantage of its range and anti-materiel properties during the First Gulf War, using it for long-range overwatch as well as targeting enemy vehicles and installations. Also appearing in the later 1980s was McMillan's TAC-50, which like the M88 offered an effective range of about 1,800m (1,969yd) (with appropriate optics), plus the formidable on-target destructive effects of the .50-caliber round. Navy SEALs took to the TAC-50, and eventually the weapon was officially adopted in the 2000s, designated the Mk 15 Mod 0. The TAC-50 was a bolt-operated weapon, working from a five-round detachable magazine, McMillan trading off rate of fire for the long-range precision that tends to come with bolt-action designs. It featured one of McMillan's fiberglass stocks, with an integral bipod (intended as the rifle's only firing mount). The 29in heavy match-grade barrel terminated in a sizable muzzle brake, necessary given the weapon's recoil. Total weight for this package was 26lb. The Mk 15 Mod 0 is still in service with the SEALs, and in 2012 the A1 and A1-R2 variants were issued, the former with an improved stock design and the latter incorporating a hydraulic recoil mitigation system into the A1 design.

McMillan sniper rifles

From the 1990s, McMillan began to field a new series of sniper rifles, all based upon its respected G30 bolt-action mechanism. The three models were the TAC-300 in .300 Winchester Magnum, the TAC-308 in 7.62×51mm, and the TAC-338 in .338 Lapua. All of the rifles work from five-round magazines. As befits a sniper rifle, the TAC series features heavy, free-floating match-grade barrels, and the fiberglass chassis has a fixed butt and adjustable cheekpiece and buttpad, with the option of a bipod fitting at the forend. Note that the TAC-308 is described by

McMillan as being for urban use, with a 24in barrel as opposed to the 27in barrel on the TAC-338 and the 26in barrel on the TAC-300. The SEALs appear to have been the primary users of the TAC series, utilizing them in combat from operations in Mogadishu in 1993 through to recent actions in Afghanistan.

The Mk 13 Mod 0

Another SOCOM sniper product of the late 1980s was the Mk 13 Mod 0. The background to this weapon was a SOCOM request for a version of the Mk 24 rifle that could fire the more powerful .300 Winchester Magnum cartridge, which had entered use in 1963 and become an especially popular hunting round. The heart of the weapon is actually the Remington 700 long bolt-action, a mechanism noted for its reliability and, through consistent and secure seating of the rounds, long-range accuracy. The Mk 13 Mod 0 has a barrel length of 26.5in, a five-round magazine, and can command ranges of up to 1,200m (1,312yd), optics and ammunition depending.

The Mk 13 Mod 0 became a favorite among Navy SEALs and MARSOC, and since it entered service its capabilities have been enhanced by a series of variant upgrades – at the time of writing, we are currently at the Mod 7 variant. Most of the variants take the KAC Mk 11 suppressor; and the Mod 5 variant utilized the Accuracy International Chassis System (AICS), a polymer and alloy chassis made by the eponymous British company to provide a stable platform for barrel and action mounting, plus full dimensions adjustability and rail mounting. The Mod 7 variant has either the SureFire SOCOM762-RC or the Advanced Armament Mk 13-SD suppressor, and firing Mk 248 match-grade ammunition it has registered kills out to 2,000m (2,188yd).

The M2010 ESR

Firing the powerful .300 Winchester Magnum, the M2010 Enhanced Sniper Rifle (ESR) entered service with the US Army in 2011, spreading out into some parts of the SOF community. The rationale behind the design was to extend the reach of snipers operating in the wide-open mountains and

This Green Beret of the 7th Special Forces Group (A) is operating an M2010 Enhanced Sniper Rifle during a shooting competition. He is making adjustments to the Leupold Mk 4 6.5–20×50mm Extended Range/Tactical M5 scope. (DoD photo by US Army Master Sgt Alex Licea)

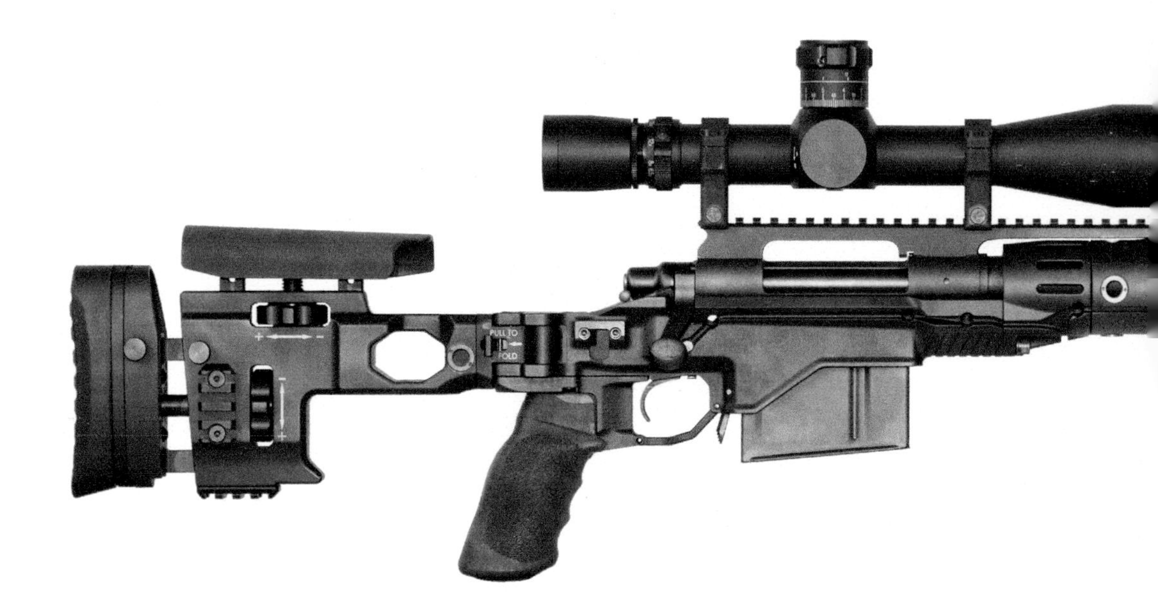

The M2010 Enhanced Sniper Rifle. (Photo Courtesy of PEO Soldier/Wikimedia/Public Domain)

plains of Afghanistan. The standard Army sniper weapon prior to the M2010 was the M24 Sniper Weapon System (SWS), which had an effective range of *c.*800m (875yd). The M2010 takes the effective range up to 1,200m (1,312yd), courtesy of the powerful cartridge plus the 24in hammer-forged free-floating barrel. It is a bolt-action weapon, fed from a five-round box magazine. Its most distinctive visual feature is the skeleton-type stock assembly, which is fully adjustable to fit precisely to the body dimensions of the shooter. The design also keeps the weapon's overall weight within manageable limits – total weight is 12.1lb. In SOCOM use, the M2010 is being replaced with the Mk 21 Precision Sniper Rifle (PSR).

The Mk 21 PSR

In February 2009, SOCOM issued a "Sources Sought Synopsis" to support "a requirement for a Precision Sniper Rifle (PSR)," noting that "The Government is interested in analyzing and testing sniper weapon systems to possibly replace the currently fielded Bolt Action SOF Sniper Systems (MK13, M40, M24)" (US Special Operations Command 2009). The long list of requirements for this weapon included either manual or gas action, 1.0 MOA accuracy at ranges of 300–1,500m (328–1,640yd), overall length no greater than 52in excluding suppressor, and the ability for the user to break it down in less than two minutes, reassembling it with no loss of zero.

In March 2013, the Remington Modular Sniper Rifle (MSR) was officially adopted to meet the PSR requirement. Subsequently relabeled the Mk 21 Precision Sniper Rifle (PSR), the defining feature of this weapon is its quick-change free-floating barrel, which allows the operator to swap barrels and calibers in a matter of minutes, the caliber options being 7.62×51mm NATO, .300 Winchester Magnum, and .338 Lapua Magnum, thus offering the ultimate in sniper modularity. Other features

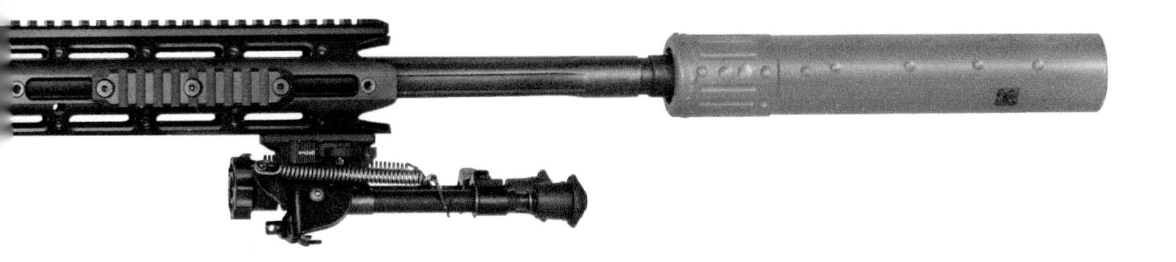

of the weapon include an AAC muzzle brake which can take a TiTAN-QD suppressor, an X-Treme Shooting adjustable trigger unit, and a removable buttstock.

MACHINE GUNS

The machine guns used by SOCOM forces to a large extent reflect those in service the wider American forces, so only some notable exceptions will be analyzed here. The legacy weapons from the Vietnam era were the modular but unreliable Stoner 63 system, of which scarcely any remained in service by the 1980, the classic M60, plus (at the heavy end) the .50-caliber Browning M2HB. While the Browning has remained an old faithful until the present day, from the 1980s SOCOM reevaluated its machine-gun requirements, and either adopted weapons outside the regular US military arsenal or adapted issue weapons to suit its own purposes.

The M60E3/M60E4/Mk 43 Mod 0

Fielded around 1986, the M60E3 was an updated version of the 7.62mm gas-operated M60, with improvements over the original version that included a better bipod, a simplified gas system, a carrying handle on the barrel, and two barrel types (lightweight and heavy). The subsequent version, the M60E4, was extensively reworked when compared to the M60E3. In addition to many internal modifications to improve reliability, a front grip was added for tactical handling, the buttstock and bipod were changed, and in addition to the long and short barrels an "assault" barrel was provided, measuring 37in. In US Navy service the M60E4 was designated the Mk 43 Mod 0.

A Navy SEAL with a Mk 43 Mod 0 machine gun. The M60 weapons series has a cyclical rate of fire of 500–600rd/min, feeding from 250-round disintegrating-link belts. (US DoD)

The M60E3 and the Mk 43 Mod 0 were both used by Navy SEALs, the latter weapon replacing the former from the mid-1990s as it became available. These weapons have served on until the present day, although in most cases they have been replaced by the FN-model weapons outlined below.

The HK21

During the 1980s and 1990s, the US Army's Delta Force and US Navy SEALs invested in stocks of an alternative to the M60 as a general-purpose machine gun: the Heckler & Koch HK21. The HK21 was a contrast to the M60 both inside and out. Its operating mechanism was not gas, but rather the roller-delayed blowback system for which Heckler & Koch was renowned. The receiver was a modified version of that from the G3 battle rifle, fitted with a detachable bipod, and feed was via belt, box, or drum for tactical or sustained-fire options. With a closed bolt and a free-floating barrel, the HK21 was extremely accurate, and it was physically light and manageable. Little wonder therefore that the founder of Delta Force, Charles Beckwith, referred to it as the "Rolls-Royce" of machine guns. The HK21 appears to have persisted in SOCOM use throughout the 1980s and into the 1990s, although it was eventually replaced by FN-model weapons.

The Mk 46 Mod 0 and Mk 48 Mod 0

The FN Minimi is one of the great success stories of modern small arms, adopted into general US service as the M249 Squad Automatic Weapon (SAW) in 1984. However, although the weapon was portable and capable of decent suppressive firepower, the standard M249 did not quite meet the requirements of many SOCOM units, and thus the Mk 46 Mod 0 was developed, then adopted in 1998.

The chief priorities in the Mk 46 redesign were enhancements to portability and accessorization. The Mk 46 Mod 0 had a barrel length of 16.3in, in between that of the standard SAW and its short Para version, and it removed the carrying handle, tripod-mounting lug, and the magazine well for optional magazine feed. The fold-down bipod can also be detached to save weight. All told, the physical trimmings reduced the weight of the Mk 46 Mod 0 by about 2lb compared to the standard M249. The Mk 46 and M249 variants have become standard issue across all SOCOM units, overcoming some reliability issues during deployments in Iraq and Afghanistan. There is also a 7.62×51mm variant, the Mk 48, which entered SOCOM service in 2000. Like the Mk 46, the Mk 48 has proved to be a popular weapon, not least because it is significantly lighter than its nearest service alternative, the M240.

Navy SEAL Petty Officer 2d Class Michael A. Monsoor was posthumously awarded the Medal of Honor on April 8, 2008, for the act of falling on a grenade on September 29, 2006 while serving in Ramadi, Iraq, thus saving the lives of his comrades. Monsoor is here armed with a Mk 46 machine gun, while the SEAL behind and to the right has a Mk 14 EBR. (Undated photo courtesy of Monsoor family/DoD)

The M240

The 7.62×51mm FN MAG has been one of the world's most successful post-World War II machine guns, adopted by more than 80 countries, including the United States as the M240. The MAG/M240 is a true general-purpose machine gun: built with the rugged construction quality that ensures reliability; simple to operate; adaptable for a range of mounts, from bipods to vehicle pintle mounts; capable of delivering extremely heavy fire at up to 900rd/min over ranges of 2,000m (2,188yd).

In 2011, SOCOM troops began trials with a new version of the M240, the M240L. This lightened and shorter variant took the barrel length down from 24.8in to 20.8in, fitted a collapsible stock, and used titanium construction to significantly lighten the weapon – total weight reduction over the standard Army M240B is 5lb – and reduce the overall length by 7in. The M240L is now integrated into SOCOM arsenals and indications are that it is a respected addition to the firepower spectrum.

This impressive photograph shows a four-man SEAL team, three of whom are armed with the 7.62×51mm Mk 48 Mod 0 machine gun. The man second from right has a Block II SOPMOD M4A1 with an ELCAN Specter DR scope. Note that at the time of writing SOCOM is starting to look for a new machine gun to replace, in some units, both the M240 and the Browning M2HB. This effort, known as the Lightweight Medium Machine Gun program, is currently paying much attention to the SIG Sauer Lightweight Machine Gun (SLMG), chambered in .338 Norma Magnum. (US DoD photo by Petty Officer 1st Class Martine Cuaron)

COMBAT SHOTGUNS

Combat shotguns are exclusively used for CQB, on account of their very limited range of about 50m (55yd). The principal value of the combat shotgun is as a breaching tool – using slugs to shoot off door locks and hinges to gain entry – but also its power as a take-down weapon. Unlike a pistol or carbine, precise shot placement is not an absolute necessity with a shotgun firing 12-gauge 00 buckshot – the multiple balls and the shot spread will mean that a single hit nearly anywhere on the enemy's torso is likely to result in near-immediate incapacitation. Magazine capacity is very limited, however, usually about seven rounds (plus one in the chamber), so the shotgun-carrying soldier needs the close protection of his carbine-carrying associates.

In the early years of SOCOM, residual stocks of Ithaca 37, Remington 870, and Mossberg 500 pump-action shotguns were carried, sometimes modified from a conventional stock to a pistol grip. While the Ithaca 37 is largely forgotten, the Remington 870 and Mossberg 500 remain in use with US SOF. The Remington 870's variant list is bewildering in its diversity, but one of the prominent SOCOM versions is the M870 Modular Combat Shotgun (MCS), which came into service in 2004. The modular features in this shotgun's title include options for three barrel lengths – 10in, 14in, and 18in – options for three different stocks, an Accessory Rail System, and two different lengths of magazine tube. The main Mossberg shotgun in SOCOM is the M590, which features internal modifications to enhance reliability, a top-mounted ambidextrous safety, railed forends, and six-position adjustable stocks. The M590A1 version also includes Picatinny top rails, Parkerized or Marinecote finishes on heavy-walled barrels, and a variety of tactical sighting options, such as ghost-ring or red-dot sights.

A popular alternative to the pump-action shotguns is the gas-operated semi-automatic Benelli M4, which was adopted as the M1014 Joint Service Combat Shotgun in 1999. Although theoretically the semi-automatic shotgun does not have the reassuring simplicity of the pump-action shotgun, the M1014 demonstrates impressive reliability, with a parts life of 25,000 rounds. Reloading time is reduced, and the gas mechanism softens felt recoil, allowing for quicker follow-up shots. A MIL-STD-1913 Picatinny sight rail on top allows use of both conventional and night-vision sights.

The M26 Modular Accessory Shotgun System (MASS) entered service with US military forces in 2006. This ingenious 12- gauge module, which has a straight-pull bolt-action and a five-round detachable box magazine, is essentially an underbarrel fitting for the M14/M16. Yet it can be detached from the shotgun and fitted with a pistol grip and collapsible stock to make it a standalone weapon. Fielding to US Army units began in 2010, but as yet it is uncertain to what extent it will be used by SOCOM units in large quantities. Nevertheless the principle of total modularity is likely to appeal to SOF, although weight considerations remain an issue for the generally light-traveling elite operators.

USE

SOCOM small arms in action

Regardless of the accuracy and firepower of any of the firearms discussed in this book, technologies count for little unless the SOCOM operator has mastered the fundamentals of weapon handling to the highest degree. Underpinning many of the following discussions and historical examples are some physical principles of firearms that are worth explaining briefly at the outset; for while SOCOM operators are sometimes ascribed with near-mythical weapons-handling skills, with entire books written to reveal the "secrets" of SOF tactical shooting, in reality SOCOM troops have simply taken basic techniques to a higher level of fluidity than normal, primarily through more time spent on the range with indulgent levels of ammunition expenditure. As a startling example of the disparity in range time between US SOF troops and conventional infantry (the latter working under greater budgetary constraints because of the volume of soldiers), it is said that in the first few years after the formation of Delta Force in 1977, the new unit expended more .45 ACP pistol ammunition than did the entire US Army (Neville 2015: 38). There are two principal differences between troops belonging to SOCOM and regular forces: first, the SOCOM troops undergo far more intensive firearms training programs, involving almost daily range time and greater ammunition consumption than regular infantry; and second, there is an acute emphasis on tactical realism in SOCOM training, including a high percentage of live-fire exercises in close proximity to other personnel to induce greater stress levels and acclimatization to both risk and proximate gunfire.

The actual specifications of the various SOCOM training programs are largely not available publicly, although we can get glimpses of the qualification criteria through advanced standard military courses (which are often run by SOF personnel), through private courses run by ex-SOF personnel, and even in the world of civilian competition shooting,

CQB qualification training with Navy SEALs. This image provides a good illustration of the proper firing stance, with knees bent to provide cushioning against recoil and to allow smooth walking movements that don't disrupt aim. (US Navy photo by Mass Communication Specialist 2d Class Erika N. Jones)

particularly the sport known variously as Practical Shooting or Action Shooting. SOCOM has especially focused its firearms training development on CQB tactics, DM capabilities, and on sniper instruction. For CQB, for example, the US Special Forces developed the Special Forces Advanced Urban Combat (SFAUC) course in the early 2000s; a 15-day program attended by ODAs, and designed to raise their general CQB skills. The program involves intensive firearms-handling elements, both carbine and handgun, plus shotgun (primarily for aggressive door-entry procedures), applied to urban terrain settings, the training including numerous shoothouse actions, room-clearance exercises, and stoppage/transition drills, all packaged within complex operational planning. In contrast to the SFAUC course, the Naval Special Warfare or SEAL sniper course runs for a total of three months, the extended curriculum not only reflecting the advanced long-range weapon skills the shooter has to possess, but also the considerable field craft and reconnaissance demands that come with being a sniper, as opposed to a DM.

All SOF units have their own training approach to firearms, but the output of each of the programs is the same. The cumulative effect of simply firing more and handling the weapons for longer, all under high-level supervision and instruction, is that SOCOM operators acquire the deep-seated "muscle memory" of every aspect of firearms handling, meaning that they often use their weapons with a fluidity and speed that enemy forces cannot match.

SHOOTING TECHNIQUES AND SHOT PLACEMENT

The manner in which SOF troops are trained to target the enemy physically has changed somewhat over the decades of SOCOM's existence. From the 1940s, various military and police authorities searched for the most effective means of utilizing firearms to disable an opponent as quickly as possible. Although Hollywood movies would have us believe otherwise, this is actually not a straightforward matter. Unless a person is hit directly through the skull or spinal column, resulting in immediate neural shutdown, people rarely drop down dead after being shot. Instead, the primary mechanism of incapacitation is blood-volume shock (reduction in blood pressure due to bleeding), and this is grimly achieved by putting multiple rounds into the center mass of the torso, where there is the greatest concentration of vital organs and blood vessels. Bleeding out takes time – even a person hit directly in the heart can still function, and fire, for several seconds if he or she is running on enough adrenaline – which is why multiple shots are required. While the caliber of the weapon does have some bearing on the process of incapacitation, the reality that most SOF soldiers have come to ackowledge is that ultimately it is accurate shot placement that is the overriding factor which decides how long an enemy remains on his or her feet.

Tactical handling of both handguns and long arms in the SOF community has been based on finding the optimal technique for delivering the fastest incapacitation within the accuracy limits of the firearm. At the beginning of SOCOM's history, one of the classic techniques advocated (especially for handguns) was the "double tap." The double tap consists of two shots delivered in very quick succession to the center mass of the opponent, the original theory being that one shot was rarely enough, but two shots would be sufficient to inflict a severe wound and achieve rapid take-down. The double tap originated in the 1930s with the combat theories of the great William Ewart Fairbairn and Eric A. Sykes, theories they proved in practice during their service in the Shanghai Police, and which were subsequently refined in the 1970s by American experts, such as former US Marine Jeff Cooper, arguably the "father" of modern handgun shooting technique. The double tap was also known to be a favored practice among the British Special Air Service (SAS).

The influence of Cooper and the synergy between British and American SOF training methods ensured that the double tap was embedded into SOCOM thinking from its earliest days. This is evident in Eric L. Haney's revealing work *Inside Delta Force*, as one of the unit's founding members. His description of early Delta Force firearms' training is fascinating not just for the training content, but also for the weapons Delta Force initially used. For example, the two primary long arms used by the trainees were a match-grade M14 rifle and the .45 ACP M3 "Grease Gun," the latter an astonishingly crude weapon for an elite unit but one that Haney came to appreciate for its decisive close-range killing power. (Haney explains that the main reason Delta Force initially used the M3 was that the unit's founder, Colonel Charles Beckwith, had managed to acquire a free consignment of the weapons from the Central Intelligence Agency.) The M3 was later replaced by the MP5, but some M3s were kept in stock, mainly for suppressed work. For handguns, the unit used the traditional .45 ACP M1911.

During their initial firearms training, Delta Force trainees focused upon single aimed shots over a variety of ranges, concentrating on accurate shot placement and deep-seated familiarity with their weapons' operation. When they were skilled in the basics, the trainees progressed to double-tap shooting, again over multiple ranges, working up their speed, moving the sights back on target rapidly out of the recoil of the first shot. A notable point regarding this training phase is that Haney, and the other operators, all developed blisters and then calluses in the web of the thumb, due to the constant handling of the powerful recoil of the M1911. This physical mark of Delta Force membership illustrates why many units in the US SOF community moved away from the big .45 ACP handgun in favor of the 9×19mm weapons.

Once double-tap shooting was mastered – typical range time was eight hours a day – then the trainees moved on to shooting on the move, firing in teams, and also performing transitions between pistol and SMG. Haney notes that the main method of pistol shooting taught was "instinctive" shooting, which is particularly suited to fast CQB. During instinctive-shooting engagements, the shooter has no time to perform careful sight alignment with the target, nor to slowly squeeze the trigger. Instead, the shooter locks his eyesight on the target, aligns the weapon naturally and intuitively, and pulls the trigger quickly, snapping out rounds and adjusting fire based on observed impact. Haney likens the technique to that used in bird shooting, in which a bird breaks from cover and the shooter has almost no time to fire a considered shot, instead just swinging the weapon up to the shoulder and pulling the trigger at roughly the right moment. These skills were practiced in the "Shooting House," a stark, dark, and ballistically proofed building in which the Delta Force trainees practiced close-range urban assaults and room-clearance drills, specifically for counterterrorism and hostage-rescue scenarios.

There is no doubt that the early Delta Force training produced a group of individuals utterly familiar with their firearms and the capabilities thereof. Yet the subsequent years have produced some significant changes in the general approach to combat marksmanship, both within SOCOM and the wider US military forces. One of the best illustrations of this shift is the instruction given in the 1993 version of the US Army's Field Manual 90-10-1, which included a new section in the Appendices called "Close Quarters Combat Techniques" (Appendix K). The authors arrange the techniques of combat aiming into a descending hierarchy:

> **c. Aim.**
> The four aiming techniques all have their place during combat in built-up areas, but the aimed quick-kill technique is the one most often used in close quarters combat.
>
> *(1) Slow aimed fire.* This technique is the most accurate. It consists of taking up a steady, properly aligned sight picture and squeezing off rounds. It is normally used for engagements beyond 25 meters [27yd] or when the need for accuracy overrides speed.
> *(2) Rapid aimed fire.* This technique features an imperfect sight picture in which windage is critical but elevation is of lesser importance. When the front sight post is in line with the target, the gunner squeezes the trigger. This technique is used against targets out to 15 meters [16yd] and is fairly accurate and very fast.

A Navy SEAL demonstrates the 9mm Heckler & Koch MP5-N submachine gun. His thumb is coming up to the selector switch, which is here set on "Safe"; the click above is semi-automatic fire, and full-automatic is above that. (US Navy photo by Photographer's Mate 1st Class (SW) Arlo Abrahamson)

> *(3) Aimed quick kill.* This technique consists of using a good spot weld and placing the front sight post flush on top of the rear peep sight. It is used for very quick shots out to 12 meters [13yd]. Windage is important, but elevation is not critical with relation to the target. This technique is the fastest and most accurate. With practice, soldiers can become deadly shots at close range.
> *(4) Instinctive fire.* This technique is the least desirable. The gunner focuses on the target and points the weapon in the target's general direction, using muscle memory to compensate for lack of aim. This technique should be used only in emergencies. (Department of the Army 1993: K-20)

The rating of "instinctive fire" as the "least desirable" option is interesting when compared with the early Delta Force training described above. We can make some allowance here for the difference between theory and practice; as we shall see below, under conditions of combat adrenaline, even the most well-trained soldier can revert to highly reactive forms of fire in an effort to stay alive. Yet if we were to draw out an admittedly very rough evolution of SOF shooting techniques and training, it would reveal that targeting has become more varied, not just to center mass, and also that generally training emphasizes continual rounds on target – not just a "double tap – observe" method – with the fire continuing until the target is effectively immobilized.

Several factors have driven these changes. First, since the late 1990s it has become increasingly common for enemy forces to wear body armor of some variety. In an interview in June 2017, Lieutenant General Robert S. Walsh, the Commanding General, Marine Corps Combat Development Command, stated that "We're seeing more body armor wherever our Marines and soldiers deploy – more of it and better quality, or better capability" (quoted in Schgol 2017).

This statement was made at a time when the Marine Corps Systems Command was working alongside SOCOM to develop the new (and ultimately controversial) M885A1 Enhanced Performance Round, a penetrator round that offers a possible solution to the problem of body armor. Yet there have also been tactical responses to body armor. Instead of SOF soldiers automatically going for the center mass, modern training equally emphasizes taking head shots as a matter of priority in CQB. Even the general-issue FM 90-10-1 recognizes this reality:

> In close quarters combat, enemy soldiers must be incapacitated immediately. Shots that merely wound or that are mortal but do not incapacitate the target instantaneously are only slightly better than clean misses. Members of clearing teams should concentrate on achieving solid, well-placed head shots. This shot placement is difficult for some soldiers to learn, having been taught previously to aim at center of mass. (Department of the Army 1993: K-20)

Furthermore, testimony from ex-SOF soldiers has pointed to a new CQB shooting technique, that of making the initial point of aim the pelvic girdle, pumping multiple shots into the lower abdomen, below the lower edge of any frontal body armor plate, to collapse the enemy's legs from under him. As he drops, his head comes forward and the operator can finish the job with a head shot.

While instinctive fire can, and will always, be a key part of any SOF soldier's tactical tool kit, the capacity to deliver more accurate fire has undoubtedly been transformed by the widespread use of advanced optics on the latest generation of carbines and assault rifles. Iron sights still very much have their place in SOF training, as optics can be damaged relatively easily by the knocks and bumps of the battlefield, at which point the well-trained soldier should seamlessly transition to the iron sights. Indeed, some SOF soldiers utilize the multi-rail setup of the modern carbine to fit dual sets of iron sights, one on top of the receiver and one along the right-hand rail (for a right-handed shooter), one sight set to medium ranges (e.g. 183m/200yd) while the other is set for CQB distances. To switch between the two, the shooter simply cants the gun through 90 degrees to the left to access the side-mounted sight, a firing technique that takes much practice to realize but which can be achieved.

The optics as provided in the SOPMOD packages have revolutionized tactical shooting. A red-dot sight such as the Eotech 553 HOLOgraphic Weapon Sight, for example, if properly zeroed, requires nothing more than the soldier to place the dot precisely on the part of the target he wishes to hit, and pull the trigger. (More about optics capabilities is discussed below.) Furthermore, the carbines and assault rifles used tend to have excellent recoil-control properties, with muzzle brakes, heavy recoil springs, and straight-in-line configurations resulting in relatively little muzzle climb. (Straight-in-line refers to the barrel, top of the receiver, and top of the stock running almost in a straight line back to the shooter's shoulder, meaning that most of the forces of recoil travel in a direct route back into the shooter's shoulder, rather than in an upward climb.) The accuracy of these weapons is especially good when using semi-automatic fire, the preferred option for most combat situations.

A member of ODA 0114, 10th Special Forces Group, fires a Glock 19 pistol during a joint training op with Hungarian special forces. One reason for the Glock's popularity is the angle of the grip, steeper than many other handguns, which makes for an instinctive "punch" forward with the fist when aiming. (US Air Force photo by Staff Sgt Tyler Placie/Released)

So today's SOF operator is far more likely to fire multiple shots at a variety of body areas, although the torso remains the target of choice if possible, for the simple reason that it is the largest part of the body and easiest to hit. The days of the double tap are, if not gone, then at least heavily modified. Now it is a common training approach to put five, six, or more rounds into the target, either in pairs or straight through. This weight of fire ensures that the enemy goes down as quickly as possible – a critical consideration these days when the combatant might also be wearing a bomb vest, be driving a vehicle-borne IED, or could be dialing the detonation of a remote explosive device on his cell phone.

PISTOL HANDLING

The use of handguns in the SOCOM community is the subject of much misunderstanding among the wider public, partly as a result of the unrealistic expectations generated by Hollywood sensationalism when it comes to handgun technique. Although an expert pistol-shot on a quiet range could put rounds into a human-sized target at up to 45m (49yd), in reality the true practical range of a handgun is more in the region of 23m (25yd) and below. At ranges of roughly 4.5–18m (4.9–20yd), the shooting is aimed, such that there is a conscious use of the sights to achieve target alignment. The grip is almost invariably double-handed, to achieve maximum lateral stability and optimize recoil control, thereby giving the greatest accuracy of fire from a short-barreled weapon.

This is not to say, however, that single-handed shooting is not taught or used in SOF. A key component of SOF handgun training is to use the handgun single-handed from either hand, so that the weapon can be guided around cover (such as the corner of a wall) that fully protects the side of the user's body. A single-handed grip is also relevant to very confined environments, such as below deck on a ship, where one hand might be gripping a flashlight and the other the handgun, or for hostage-rescue actions in which a lead member of the entry team might be carrying a ballistic shield with one hand, with a handgun in the other aimed around the edge of the shield. The other instance where a single-handed grip might be used is in the case of a rapid draw at very short ranges – e.g. less than 4.5m (5yd) – where the speed of the encounter means that there isn't sufficient time for either aiming carefully or adopting a professional shooting stance. In these cases, the gun might be fired "Wild West" style from the hip, the elbow and forearm being pressed hard against the side of the body to generate some stability for the weapon. Less violently, a single-handed grip might be used when physically controlling a suspect with the other hand.

US SOF troops spend endless hours performing what are termed "transition drills." During a firefight, if the primary weapon (typically a carbine or assault/battle rifle) experiences a stoppage, ideally the shooter will find the time and cover sufficient to clear the problem and reenter the firefight with his "primary." If the threat is immediate, however, and the soldier needs to maintain his fire, then the primary weapon is released and allowed to hang from the sling and the "secondary" (handgun) is quickly drawn and brought into action. When a safe moment presents itself, the soldier should then return his handgun to its holster and clear the primary weapon.

A textbook example of the transition drill in action is found in former Navy SEAL Mark Owen's *No Hero: The Evolution of a Navy SEAL.* In this book, Owen recounts his first operational deployment with SEAL Team Five to war-torn Baghdad. His team was tasked with apprehending a former Iraqi Air Force intelligence officer in a night raid on the wanted man's compound. The team deployed fast to the front of the building by Humvee, and a breaching charge blew off the front door, allowing the team to enter. The fugitive was quickly captured, but then blasts of AK fire came from the top of the building's staircase, ripping into the foyer. To disorientate the opponent, the SEALs hurled nonlethal stun grenades up the stairs; then Owen and a comrade advanced up the stairs into the smoke, firing rounds as they went to provide a semblance of covering fire.

Afghanistan, 2010 (opposite)

Two Navy SEALs, visiting a rural village on an intelligence-gathering operation, are unexpectedly confronted by a Taliban assailant, who reaches for his weapon in the interior of the house. The lead SEAL, his Mk 17 Mod 0 SCAR-H (Special Operations Forces Combat Assault Rifle – Heavy) hanging by the sling at his side, reaches quickly for his 9mm SIG Sauer P226 pistol, moving straight into a double-handed combat stance and flicking on his tactical light to illuminate the target, which is neutralized with a close-range head shot. Meanwhile, his comrade brings his Mk 16 Mod 0 SCAR up into his shoulder and takes aim on the target, looking through his EOTech optical sight with switch-to-side magnifier; the Mk 17 Mod 0 SCAR-H is fitted with a Schmidt & Bender ShortDot optical sight. Both rifles are also fitted with AN/PEQ-15 Advanced Target Pointer/Illuminator/Aiming Laser (ATPIAL) devices. These transmit both infrared and visible laser illumination, making them very useful for night combat using the infrared with night-vision systems, or for CQB in darkened rooms and corridors using the visible laser light.

A Navy SEAL diver transitions out of the water and onto the beach with his 9mm SIG Sauer P226 pistol at the ready. Ideally the handgun should be drained of water before firing, to avoid the risk of barrel explosion due to overpressure. (DoD photo by Senior Chief Petty Officer Andrew McKaskle, US Navy)

After discharging four rounds, Owen's M4A1 jammed, and noting that there was no time to effect a clearance drill, he automatically let his carbine hang from the strap and drew his pistol, using this weapon to cover the rest of his ascent of the stairs and into the hallway above. Realizing that the gunman had apparently absconded, Owen found a place to holster his pistol and clear the jam in his primary weapon.

Although the SOCOM operator should never automatically rely on a handgun as his primary weapon, the specialist nature of SOF operations means that there are occasions when handguns take on a more offensive aspect. Indeed, at the end of the 1980s SOCOM launched its Offensive Handgun Weapon System (OHWS) program, the objective of which was to find or develop a handgun that could adopt primary weapon status for certain missions. Whatever weapon was chosen, it had to be resilient (including high resistance to corrosion), reliable, and, most important, had to be hard-hitting regarding terminal ballistics. For this latter reason, 9×19mm was rejected as a caliber option, regarded as too weak. Conversely, the 10mm Auto being explored for FBI adoption was dismissed as being too powerful; unlike law-enforcement guns, military SOF-spec weapons had to be capable of handling many thousands of training rounds, and the 10mm Auto would overstress semi-automatic mechanisms. Thus .45 ACP was the caliber chosen, albeit with a souped-up +P loading.

By August 1991, two handguns were in the Phase I competition: what would become the Heckler & Koch Mk 23 and Colt's offering, the Colt OHWS. The latter was modeled very directly on the Colt M1911, but with a ten-round magazine, a decocking mechanism, and a rotating barrel locking mechanism. Ultimately the OHWS did not beat the Mk 23 to win the prize, but the fact that both pistols were chambered for .45 ACP illustrates how even though shot placement can be the most critical factor in the incapacitation of an enemy, the 9mm round was not considered worthy in a weapon that might take *primary* status in a close-quarters fight.

A Navy SEAL practices his marksmanship with a Harris bipod-stabilized M4A1 Carbine, fitted with a KAC sound suppressor, an Insight Technology AN/PEQ-2 ITPIAL illuminator, and a Trijicon Advanced Combat Optical Gunsight (ACOG). (US Navy photo by Photographer's Mate 1st Class (SW) Arlo Abrahamson)

CARBINE/RIFLE HANDLING

Studying photographs of SOF troops over the last 30 years of SOCOM, one is struck by an apparent shift in the way that carbines are physically handled. In the early days of SOCOM, the stance and grip are what we might think of as "traditional" – the body angled or "bladed" at 45 degrees or more to the target; feet shoulder-width apart with the lead foot advanced; head on the stock naturally aligned with the sights; rifle mounted naturally in the pocket of the shoulder; elbows tucked down; front supporting hand usually either just in front of the magazine well or at the midpoint on the weapon's forend. Modern SOF troops, however, often display distinct differences in stance – body "flatter" and presented forward with less of an angle; rifle stock placed more toward the center of the chest; head often lifted from the stock to access optical-sight alignment; front supporting hand extended well forward, often to a point just behind the muzzle.

The latter stance is actually more specifically related to CQB settings. Part of the reason for its evolution is the rise of tactical competition shooting in the United States, in which competitive shooters have to switch rapidly

Paktika Province, Afghanistan, 2011 (overleaf)

Delta Force soldiers conducting an operation in southeast Paktika Province, Afghanistan, 2011, engage in a heavy firefight with Taliban forces, moving quickly to positions of cover amid a rocky, mountainous landscape. The soldier in the foreground is armed with a Mk 48 Mod 0 machine gun, fitted with an ELCAN Specter DR scope. The weapon is feeding from a 100-round ammunition bag, and the rate of fire is *c.*700rd/min. His comrades are armed with HK416 rifles fitted with Schmidt & Bender ShortDot optical sights and AN/PEQ-15 ATPIAL illuminator systems. The rifles also have Advanced Armament Corp. suppressors. Although the suppressors only reduce the sound of the fire moderately, it is sufficient to protect the shooter's hearing to some degree (although many soldiers still wear hearing protection) and to mask the sounds of the shots in the context of a cacophony of gunfire.

SHUMATE
2019

and accurately between multiple targets at varying ranges. The drive to win led to constant innovation in grip and posture, often led by former SOF operators such as Pat McNamara (former 1SFOD), Kyle Defoor (former Navy SEAL), and Mike Pannone (former 1SFOD), who in turn brought to competition shooting their experience with tactical weapon handling – the relationship between tactical and competition shooting has been quite synergistic. One of most distinctive elements to emerge from this evolution has been the forward "C" grip: the front grip hand is extended a long way up the forend, sometimes literally wrapping around the front curve of the forend just behind the muzzle, with the thumb of the grip hand actually over the top of the weapon (hence the grip is sometimes referred to as the "thumb-over-bore"). From the forward grip, the weapon is pulled back strongly into the shoulder or upper chest, sometimes with the grip arm flared out strongly to the side, parallel with the side of the gun.

The argument for this grip is that it better controls recoil and muzzle climb, the front hold literally steadying the muzzle at source. It is also argued that this grip, when combined with a more forward-facing stance and a stock placement further toward the centerline of the chest, allows the shooter to "drive" the gun more through rooms and complex spaces, the controlled muzzle leading the way and allowing for very quick gun-to-target alignment when necessary. In a sense, "pointing" the arm at the target will bring the gun onto the target as well.

In real-world SOF contexts, the hand-forward carbine grip does seem to have utility for both recoil control and quick target acquisition. However, many SOF operators have front foregrips fitted to the underside of the weapon's forend. This becomes the front grip point, obviating the need for the C-grip hand configuration. By using the foregrip, the elbow of the forward hand can also be dropped lower; one criticism of the C-grip is that it raises the forward arm too high, thereby obscuring some of the operator's peripheral vision to the left (in the case of a right-handed shooter). Soldiers who have engaged in combat also attest to the fact that during actual firefights, particularly over long periods, natural adjustments of stance and orientation to cover mean that the grip on the weapon does

Navy SEALs assigned to Combined Joint Special Operations Task Force, Afghanistan, scan for targets with their Mk 17 SCAR-H rifles in Maiwand District, Kandahar Province, July 2012. (US Army photo by Petty Officer 1st Class Martine Cuaron)

Soldiers of the 7th Special Forces Group (A) conduct urban-warfare training armed with M4 CQBR carbines, fitted with EOTech holographic sights and tactical flashlights. (Photo by Sgt Daniel Love, 7th Special Forces Group PAO)

change naturally. Having the arm out front is indeed a good way of controlling the muzzle, but the effort of doing so can produce muscle fatigue over time, resulting in the forward hand naturally gravitating toward the magazine well. Indeed, some SOF weapon trainers allow for this, teaching a shooting stance in which the forward arm moves right in front of the magazine well, with the bent elbow of the forward arm propped against the front of the body armor, effectively creating a supported platform for the carbine.

As with the issue of caliber choice, the debates surrounding carbine grip can be vigorous, though they tend to be less so within the SOF community itself, where kinks in the system have been ironed out with actual combat experience and the personal preference of the operator. The modularity and ergonomic features of modern assault rifles mean that the operator can adapt his weapon to personalized hold preferences.

SLINGS

Slings might appear a peripheral topic in the context of SOCOM firearms, but they are actually worth a little more serious consideration. In popular understanding, a rifle sling is purely seen as a tool by which to carry the weapon, especially when the shoulder is in noncombat situations such as parade or administrative duties. In reality, intelligent configuration of the sling makes a major difference to the tactical handling of the SOCOM carbines and rifles described in this book. A sling is not – or is no longer – just a means to suspend a rifle over the shoulder.

Instead, a good sling setup facilitates combat shooting in the following ways. First, the sling should suspend the weapon securely and comfortably from the body when the soldier is not holding the firearm, allowing him to do other things with his hands. In this capacity, the sling should also work to alleviate some of the fatigue of carrying a heavy firearm for long periods of time. Second, the sling setup should allow the soldier to lift the

With an ingenious use of webbing, a Scout Sniper stabilizes his Mk 11 Mod 0 sniper rifle in the doorway of a USAF HH-60G Pave Hawk helicopter during aerial sniper training. (Photo by Lance Cpl Daniel E. Valle/ US Army)

firearm very quickly and always safely from a hanging position to a shouldered position, should the soldier have to respond to a threat. Third, if the soldier is shooting with the sling around the neck or shoulder, it should not restrict movement in any way, particularly in the prone position. Fourth, the sling can add to the control of the weapon when firing, by providing a source of dynamic tension that assists in controlling recoil and muzzle climb. Finally, the sling should allow the soldier to make smooth transitions from carbine to handgun and back again.

The slings used by SOCOM forces have not always been able to fulfill all these criteria. Jeff Gurwitch, a former soldier with the US Army's 3d and 5th Special Forces groups, served in the First Gulf War (as a member of the 1st Armored Division), did three tours of Iraq, and spent three years as an instructor at the John F. Kennedy Special Warfare Center and School. In a useful and balanced article about tactical rifle slings (Gurwitch 2011), he notes that during 1990–97 the choice of rifle sling for soldiers was generally either the traditional two-point sling, principally used for carrying the rifle over the shoulder either on the march or on the parade ground, or a homemade variant. This situation changed with the SOPMOD program in the late 1990s, which introduced a multipoint sling, also known as a three-point sling. The multipoint sling was a case, arguably, of theory being slightly out of step with reality. The sling featured a two-point strap which ran along the rifle from forend to stock, but also an additional loop with a free-running buckle (when unclipped) that slid along the side strap. The soldier placed the additional loop over his head, wearing the strap in a diagonal from the left shoulder to the right side of the waist (for a right-handed shooter). In this configuration, the weapon can be hung in a useful variety of ways simply by maneuvering it into position: down by the right hip; close-in across the chest (especially useful if the operator is riding in a vehicle and cannot have his carbine dangling at his side); or slung over his back if he needs both of his arms free. Regardless of the position, the multipoint sling's free-running buckle meant that the carbine could be brought into action quickly, automatically adjusting to the shooter's firing stance, including prone.

FIRE CONTROL AND AMMUNITION SUPPLY

For carbines and rifles, semi-automatic fire is the preferred setting on the weapon for tactical purposes, as it offers both accuracy and, with good trigger control, reasonable rapidity for suppressive effects. Full-automatic fire and three-round burst tend to be used more for outright suppression or engagement of group or area targets rather than pinpoint targets. Yet given that SOF troops frequently operate a long way from convenient resupply, relying on just the ammunition they can personally carry, reckless full-automatic fire can quickly empty magazines.

Of all the items carried by SOF troops on operations, weighting is naturally given to ammunition. Even if a SOF soldier demonstrates responsible fire control, a modern firefight tends to be extremely greedy on cartridge consumption. The load-carrying systems of SOCOM forces have principally been the Individual Integrated Fighting System (IIFS), the Modular Lightweight Load-carrying Equipment (MOLLE), and an assortment of tactical vests and body armor systems, these fitted with the Pouch Attachment Ladder System (PALS) webbing that enables much equipment to be hung from a lattice of horizontal nylon straps. For carbines and rifles, magazines are typically supported around the front waist, up to three magazines on each side, with possible additional magazines held around the lower back, within reach. Thus maximum carbine ammunition capacity tends to be in the region of 150–250 rounds, depending on the number of magazines and the number of rounds loaded into each magazine. (Experienced troops will generally refrain from loading magazines up to their maximum capacity, because this places the magazine springs under maximum tension, weakening them over time and raising the chances of malfunctions.)

One of the advantages of the commonality of 5.56×45mm and 7.62×51mm cartridges in SOCOM use is that *in extremis*, when ammunition is running low, cartridges can be stripped from belts of machine-gun ammunition to top up the rifles and carbines. Standard-issue ball ammunition, however, does not give the degree of accuracy delivered by the match-grade cartridges used in sniping and marksmen weapons, so using regular ammunition is only an emergency measure.

A Navy SEAL team member fires a Mk 43 Mod 0 machine gun during a training exercise. Firing the weapon from the shoulder, usually using the front grip, requires a heavy build and very controlled bursts if recoil isn't to throw the shooter off-balance. (PH1 CHUCK MUSSI/Wikimedia/Public Domain)

Multipoint slings still have their advocates, and they have been used extensively in combat; but generally speaking they have fallen out of favor with SOCOM troops, for the simple reason that the multiple straps are easily caught on the plethora of kit mounted on the troop's belt, chest, and back. (By way of balance, Gurwitch notes that this situation can be overcome simply through plenty of practice with the sling.)

Thus the single-point sling came into being, and this is still one of the most popular types of sling today. The single-point sling has a carrying loop that merges into a single strap which is fixed to the weapon at a single point on the stock or the rear receiver. The single-point sling has the advantage of simplicity and is both versatile and intuitive to use. It can be slung around the neck only, to hang the weapon straight down in front of the user, or it can be worn over the shoulder and chest to support the weapon down by the side. An issue that people tend to find with such slings, however, is that when hanging at the side they tend to gravitate around to the center of the body, where they bounce around under movement and interfere with actions such as going prone or climbing an assault ladder.

For these reasons, the US SOF community has seen many soldiers return to modern two-point slings, albeit that they are distinguished from the early leather versions by their use of improved fabrics and better strap adjustability. The advantage of the two-point sling is that it can be worn either around the neck or across the chest, as can the single-point sling, but the weapon tends to stay in place better once suspended. Of course, some SOCOM troops have the best of both worlds by acquiring commercial sling types that can convert between two-point and single-point setups, although the operator has to be careful, as with all slings, that any quick-release buckles are designed so as not to be released unintentionally if they snag on equipment.

FIREARM ACCESSORIES

It is important to emphasize that SOCOM troops do not, as a rule, have free choice from the world's catalogue of firearms, although that myth has been a persistent one. On rare occasions a personal weapon – usually a handgun – might be carried by the SOCOM soldier in addition to his service weapons, but in the vast majority of cases he will be equipped with the weapons as supplied in the unit arsenal. It is for this reason, however, that modularity and accessorization are critical elements in the choice of SOCOM weaponry. For example, the standard M4 carbine, stripped down to its fundamentals, is the same basic weapon throughout the US armed forces. The SOCOM soldier, however, can then draw upon the resources of the SOPMOD accessories, plus any commercial sources he sees fit, to optimize the weapon for the mission.

This Green Beret in Afghanistan, 2013, has a Mk 17 SCAR-H rifle fitted with an ELCAN Specter DR Multi-Function Combat Day Sight, an Insight Technology AN/PEQ-15 APTIAL, an Insight Technology WMX200 Visible Bright Light, and a GPSI Grip Pod foregrip/bipod. (US Army photo by Pfc David Devich/Released)

The words "for the mission" are central here. Although modern rifles are kitted out with extensive rail systems, the temptation to overload the weapon is avoided by experienced troops. The only accessories used should be those that contribute to mission success; adding unnecessary pieces of kit simply piles on the pounds that contribute steadily to muscle fatigue over the course of a long operation, and which can make the weapon slow to move in action.

When we look through photographs of typical SOF weapon setups, we see a distinct change from the late 1980s to the present day. In photographs from the early days of SOCOM, we often see SOF soldiers with unadorned weapons, shooting them over their iron sights. On occasions, we might see an operator with an early generation of Starlight or thermal-imaging scope, for night missions. As the 1990s progressed, and rail fittings collected atop receivers and around forends, increasing volumes of tactical accessories appeared, and in the 21st century, the era of the War on Terror, these volumes largely reached their practical peak. If we look at a typical modern SOF carbine setup, for example, we can divide the accessories into four main categories: optics, kinetic modules (grenade launchers), illumination, and noise suppression (suppressors).

Optics

Combat optics is a huge subject in its own right, with hundreds of different types, brands, and models, thus only an overview is possible here. It should be noted in passing that the prevalence of combat optics has not rendered iron sights redundant. As combat in World War II and numerous other wars have shown, a good set of iron sights, properly zeroed and used by a well-trained soldier, can give perfectly accurate results up to and even well beyond 275m (301yd). Iron sights do not fail in extremes of cold and heat, and they are highly resistant to damage. This is why the SOPMOD Block I accessory kit still includes back-up iron sights (BUIS), and the latest micro-aperture types have adjustability up to 600m (656yd). Some weapons, such as the Heckler & Koch rifles, feature rear diopter sights with a similar range bracket. Other iron sights include tritium illumination for low-light conditions. Given the practicality and dependability of iron sights, therefore, it would be unwise for an operator to leave these off; it is only in the case of some DM rifles and most sniper rifles that we see SOF troops without iron sights.

There is no denying, however, that modern optics can dramatically improve both target acquisition and the speed and accuracy of shooting. For CQB and medium-range work, the chief types of optics that have emerged over the last 30 years are red dot, holographic, and magnifying. With a red-dot sight, once zeroed all it takes to sight the weapon is to place the red dot on the target and pull the trigger. A key advantage of red-dot sights, and indeed holographic and all non-magnifying types, is that the shooter can use them with both eyes open, an accommodation that dramatically speeds up shooting response time. Holographic sights work by superimposing a holographic reticle

An M4A1 Carbine fitted with a Trijicon ACOG scope. Some ACOG variants include backup ghost-ring iron sights fitted to the exterior, or top-mounted reflex sights. (US Air Force photo by Tech Sgt Brian Snyder)

image at a distance on the field of view. The advantage of the holographic sight is that it works even if the shooter's eye is not squared up to the back of the sight or even aligned completely with the sight; and it can also be used perfectly well while the shooter is wearing goggles and a respirator.

While red-dot and holographic sights have certainly changed the face of personal military firepower, their principal shortcoming is that they are non-magnifying, which causes problems if the shooter suddenly has to transition from close-up targets to those in the distance. One solution is EOTech's own switch-to-side magnifier system, a magnifying optic that can literally be flipped up in front of the Aimpoint or EOTech sight to provide instant magnification, to the power of 1× or 3×, and without changing the zero of the weapon.

If the SOF soldier's mission requires a greater spectrum of range possibilities, as might be found in a war zone such as Afghanistan, then magnifying scopes are chosen. These can be of either fixed or variable magnification. Of the fixed-magnification types, one of the most popular is the Trijicon Advanced Combat Optical Gunsight (ACOG), fitted on many weapons from carbines to machine guns. The ACOG is a fixed-power (1.5× to 6×, depending on the model), compact riflescope with an illuminated reticle pattern (for use in bright to low/no light conditions) and bullet-drop compensating reticles, housed in a tough and waterproof aluminum alloy housing. Trijicon have also managed to give the ACOG a both-eyes-open design.

SOCOM SNIPING ACTION

A striking demonstration of the influence a well-equipped SOF sniper can have over the battlefield comes from a major engagement on August 8, 2008, near the village of Shewan in Farah Province, Afghanistan. On that day, elements of 2d Platoon, Golf Company, 2d Battalion, 7th Marines and 2d Platoon, 1st Force Reconnaissance Company (Force Recon), conducted a clearance operation that turned into a blistering eight-hour firefight as hundreds of Taliban clashed with a force of just a few dozen Marines. In such a clash, the Marines needed force multipliers. Some of those came from close air support (CAS), but another was the activity of Force Recon snipers, not least Corporal Franklin Simmons, armed with a Mk 11 Mod 0 sniper rifle. A group of Marines was trapped in an exposed kill zone after their Humvee was disabled by RPG and small-arms fire. Seeing the danger that the men were in, Simmons moved up onto the top of an exposed berm, a position that attracted fire but from where he had a clear line of sight to take shots with his rifle. Simmons began to fire on targets of opportunity, and such was his skill and the accuracy of his rifle that he killed 20 of the enemy. For his actions that day, Simmons was awarded the Silver Star. Although the details of each individual shot are not available, the battle of Shewan demonstrates how the semi-automatic sniper platform can be used to lethal effect in engagements where multiple targets present themselves.

A US Army Ranger performs overwatch with a Mk 11 Mod 0 sniper rifle in Baghdad, Iraq, 2006. The scope is a standard-issue Leupold type. (US Army)

Variable-magnification sights are especially useful when the expected combat ranges are less well known, as a simple lever or dial on the side of the sight can adjust the optic to suit the engagement distances. An excellent example in use by SOCOM is the Schmidt & Bender ShortDot range of 1× to 4× magnification that includes bullet-drop compensator (BDC) features. A more sophisticated option is the ELCAN Specter DR. The DR stands for "Dual Role," referring to its dual field of view – the shooter can switch the sight instantly from a 4× magnified sight to a 1× CQB sight just by flipping a lever, at the same time flipping from a standard combat distance reticle to a red dot.

When it comes to sniper rifles, the issue of optics becomes far more complex. All such sights are powerful magnifying types (fixed or variable), typically of 10× to 20× magnification, with fine range adjustment and often BDCs. Such scopes can be supported by a range of ancillary

This US Army Special Forces soldier, operating in Afghanistan alongside Afghan National Army commandos, is armed with a bipod-mounted 7.62×51mm Mk 17 Mod 0 SCAR-H. The optic is an ELCAN Specter scope. (US DoD)

This M4A1 Carbine has been fitted with the M26 12-Gauge Modular Accessory Shotgun System (MASS). As well as firing door-breaching rounds and regular shot, the MASS can fire less-lethal munitions. (Photo Courtesy of PEO Soldier/Wikimedia/Public Domain)

equipment, such as laser rangefinders. With these scopes, when allied to good rifles, the results can be formidable. The distance record for a kill by a US sniper came in March 2004, when Ranger Sgt. Bryan Kremer used a Barrett M82A1 rifle to kill an Iraqi insurgent at a distance of 2,400m (2,625yd).

Kinetic modules

Since the 40mm M203 was introduced in the late 1960s, Underslung Grenade Launchers (UGLs) have provided US troops with a force multiplier attached directly to their rifle or carbine, capable of delivering a variety of area, anti-personnel, anti-armor (limited), or obscuration/marking effects out to ranges of 400m (437yd). The two principal types

A US Special Forces soldier in Afghanistan, 2010, armed with an M4A1 fitted with an ELCAN Specter DR scope and an M203 underbarrel grenade launcher. The man to the right has an 84mm M136 AT-4 rocket launcher. (US Army photo by Spc Nicholas T. Lloyd Combined Joint Special Forces Task Force Afghanistan)

in use with SOCOM are the M203 and the M320 Grenade Launcher Module (GLM), the latter officially replacing the former in SOCOM since 2009, although it is not uncommon to find M203s soldiering on. Both fire the 40×46mm SR rounds to similar maximum ranges, but can also be carried as standalone systems when fitted with a stock and pistol grip. Both the M203 and the M320 are single-shot weapons, the M203 breech opened by sliding the serrated grip section directly forward, while the M320 breech is exposed by swinging it out to the side of the rifle; this configuration allows the M320 to take some of the new generations of 40mm shells, which are longer than the M203 can accommodate. Some of the M320's other innovations, in comparison with the M203, include a double-action trigger mechanism, sights mounted directly on the side of the launcher, and the ability to fit onto a rifle or carbine without a special mounting kit.

Illumination

Moving away from optics, we now look at illumination devices. In many SOF photographs over the last 20 years, we commonly see illumination devices attached to the forend of the weapon, for nighttime combat actions. Tactical illumination tends to present itself through three main technologies: infrared (IR) illuminators, visible laser light illuminators, and tactical flashlights. A flashlight is the least-sophisticated illumination tool, but can provide an invaluable beam of light for checking out dark areas of buildings. The beam of light can also act as a crude aiming guide over close ranges, and can even serve to blind or temporarily confuse an enemy while a shot is taken, although conversely the beam of light can act as an aiming point for return fire.

Visible laser lights are the signature red light beams so adored by the makers of action movies. In reality, they tend to be used primarily to zero weapon sights, or as a quick means of designating a target or other object for people close by. Laser light is as visible to the enemy as it is to the shooter, and it is far better for a soldier to allow a sight to guide him to the target than it is a distant and bobbing point of light; so laser pointers do not confer all the tactical advantages seen in the movies, but they are nonetheless useful.

IR illuminators work by throwing out a beam of IR light, which can then be seen through a night-vision device, such as a scope or goggles. IR illuminators offer two primary tactical advantages: first, they can literally illuminate dark corners of the battlefield that image-intensifiers might struggle to picture, especially on nights with no moonlight or starlight; and second, they provide feedback to all team members about which enemy combatant is targeted by which friendly soldier. In daylight, target allocation among team members has to be performed either with visual or verbal instructions. By contrast, an IR-illuminator-equipped team at night will literally see where everyone else is aiming, and well-trained SOF operators will automatically spread their point of aim evenly across all the target opportunities, to maximize the impact of the opening fire.

SOCOM troops are trained against using IR illuminators indiscriminately, however. The main problem comes when facing enemies who also have IR capabilities; an enemy wearing night-vision goggles (NVGs) can actually use the beams from the SOF IR illuminators to trace the operator back to source, and thus identify the target. This problem has

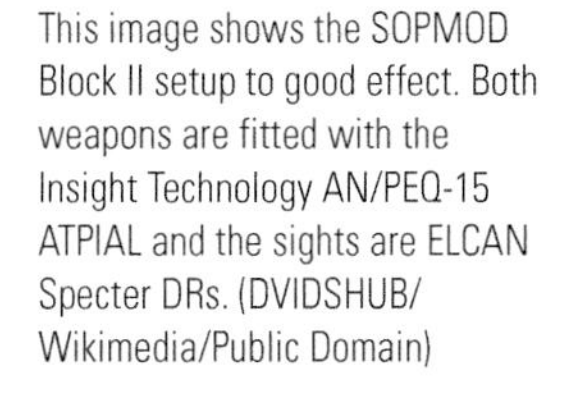

This image shows the SOPMOD Block II setup to good effect. Both weapons are fitted with the Insight Technology AN/PEQ-15 ATPIAL and the sights are ELCAN Specter DRs. (DVIDSHUB/Wikimedia/Public Domain)

A US Special Forces operator uses an infrared illuminator device (the wider beam) and an infrared target pointer (the narrower beam) to search for enemy combatants during a night operation in Afghanistan. (US Army photo by Staff Sgt Jeremy D. Crisp/Special Operations Task Force South)

become more acute over time. Winding the clock back to 1991 and the First Gulf War, the US-led Coalition's offensive to drive Iraqi forces out of Kuwait, the SOFs' advantage in night vision was near absolute during its numerous nighttime raids into Kuwait and Iraq. Former Navy Secretary John Lehman explained in a Congress hearing in 1991 that "It was the ability to attack at night, when all of the rest of the world's defenses are at 10 percent of what they are in daytime, that gave us this huge immediate impact and edge" (quoted in Raymond 2017). Yet during the War on Terror in the 21st century, it has been found that the enemy is often fully cognizant of the importance of night vision, and has often acquired sets of their own through the military black market or through direct commercial purchase. SOF operators therefore have to be far more careful in how they use their weapon-mounted IR systems. A general rule has been to apply the designators sparingly, flicking them on to illuminate and engage the target briefly, then switching them off again the moment the task has been accomplished, and quickly moving position. The same rule also applies to weapon-mounted flashlights.

IR illuminators have not only proved significant for CQB, but also for SOF snipers and marksmen. Former US Special Forces soldier Karl Erickson has explained something of the history and utility of IR illuminators, allied to sniping scopes, for long-range shooting (Erickson 2016). One of the chief advantages of IR illuminators is their ability to extend the range of target identification at night. As Erickson explains, during low-light or nighttime hours, visual acquisition with a conventional

The AN/PVS-4 Night Vision Sight, Individual Served Weapon is a second-generation night-vision device that was first used on SOF (and other units') weapons in 1978, and which through a series of modifications has remained in service, if not production, to the present day. (David_Kitson/ Wikimedia/Public Domain)

scope might only be out to 300–400m (328–437yd), but with the extra clarity provided by IR illumination the reach can be up to 700m (766yd). IR illumination also provides the added benefit of being better able to distinguish between friend and foe – a crucial advantage if SOF soldiers are to stay the right side of the rules of engagement.

In this context, Erickson makes the interesting historical point that during the Vietnam and post-Vietnam eras, the use of night-vision scopes was limited, because the resolution they offered was not good enough to provide secure target identification. That situation began to improve with the introduction of sights such as the Optic Electronics AN/PVS-4 Night Vision Sight, Individual Served Weapon, the first of the second-generation passive night-vision scopes, introduced in 1978. The AN/PVS-4 delivered a relatively high-quality image to the viewer, one free from distortion and which could compensate for changes in ambient temperature. SOCOM operators used the AN/PVS-4 through the 1980s and 1990s; it gave good service during the First Gulf War. Although production of the AN/PVS-4 was completed in 2002, the type continues in use today, and it has spawned a range of improved variants.

Today, Erickson points out, the latest third-generation sights offer such a fine resolution that it is possible for long-range shooters to see wind effects on grass and trees, enabling them to adjust their shot to accommodate environmental factors. Another bonus of the latest sights, Erickson explains, is that the spotter can actually see the "trace" of the bullet in flight as the IR illuminator lights up the rear of the bullet. (Erickson notes that this effect is dependent on the ammunition type; the Sierra MatchKing is especially suitable, as the base of the bullet is a flat copper disk that responds well to the "light up" effect of the illuminator beam.) Being able to see the bullet in flight has an important tactical benefit, in that the spotter can observe whether it has hit the enemy combatant or actually missed but driven him to take cover. Erickson notes that he has witnessed incidents in which the sniper thinks that the target has been taken out, only for the enemy to reappear suddenly and fight as the friendly troops break cover. SOCOM troops today often configure

Here we see a unit of Navy SEALs participating in a beach firing exercise. The weapons are a mix of Mk 17 Mod 0 SCAR-H rifles (fitted with FN 701 suppressors) and a Mk 46 Mod 0 machine gun. (US Navy photo by Mass Communication Specialist 2d Class Anthony Harding/ Released)

their carbines with an AN/PEQ-15 Advanced Target Pointer/Illuminator/ Aiming Laser (ATPIAL), a combined visible laser and IR illuminator device, plus a tactical flashlight, all grouped around the front end of the forend rails.

Suppressors

Suppressors are generally seen fitted either to SOF combat handguns (rarely) or carbines and rifles. The tactical purpose of a suppressor is, naturally, to lower the sound signature of the weapon when fired, as much for the benefit of the shooter's hearing as for concealability. If the suppressor is used with supersonic ammunition, the gun report is still surprisingly loud for those expecting the weak "phut" portrayed in some TV movies; using subsonic ammunition plus a suppressor will have a greater effect on the volume, but at the expense of velocity and therefore range and penetration. Another key tactical benefit of the suppressor is to reduce muzzle flash during nighttime engagements. This has the benefit of concealing the shooter's position from enemies looking for muzzle flashes, and helping to preserve the shooter's nighttime eyesight.

As we have seen from our study so far, the world of SOCOM weaponry has become very sophisticated indeed, with its emphasis on modularity and ancillary combat technologies. The question therefore arises as to whether or not these developments have had a truly appreciable impact on the outcome of combat.

IMPACT

Controlling the firefight

AFGHAN FIREFIGHT

An entry point into evaluating the impact of SOCOM small-arms development comes again from former Navy SEAL Mark Owen, who recounts from his time deployed to Afghanistan an aggressive direct-action night operation conducted by a mixed unit of Navy SEALs, Army Rangers, and some Afghan special forces (Owen 2014). While the SEALs were armed with HK416 carbines, fitted with EOTech optics and LAMs, and also the 5.56mm Mk 46 machine gun, the other troops had with them Mk 48 machine guns, which were being used to establish a base of support fire if the unit ran into heavy opposition in the enemy compound that was their objective. Thus while the machine guns established themselves in an overwatch position, the SEALs pushed down the right flank of an open field in front of the compound area, moving slowly through the thick grass and over various obstacles. A tree line around the compound held suspected enemy troops.

Owen recounts seeing, through his NVGs, the crisscross patterns of the IR illuminators mounted on the carbines, which assisted not only in targeting but also in orientating across the landscape. Suddenly, the team froze as they stumbled across a Taliban soldier sleeping in the tree line, oblivious to the lethal threat around him. The SEALs were all equipped with suppressors on their carbines, but even a suppressed gunshot would have split the stillness of the night and alerted the enemy. Thus two SEALs stayed with their weapons trained on the sleeping man, while the rest moved forward, advancing from out of the tree line onto the driveway of the compound, with clear evidence (parked cars) indicating that the compound was occupied.

With the Mk 46 gunner out to the left, the SEALs moved steadily up the compound, very aware of the threat that was likely concealed in the woodland wrapped around the house. Near the dwelling, the unit came across piles of mats and blankets on the ground, appearing as if they had been hurriedly left there. Now primed for contact, the team stopped and carefully scanned the trees with their IR illuminators. Then Owen spotted, briefly, the silhouette of a human head pop up and down in the trees, and alerted the rest of the SEALs via his radio. At that moment, a darkened figure stood up and began to unleash fire at the SEALs with a 7.62mm PKM machine gun. Two interesting points come out of Owen's narrative at this moment. One is how the strobing muzzle flash of the PKM overloaded his NVGs with light. The other is his acknowledgment that as he returned fire with his HK416 he lost focus of his optic, LAM, and iron sights – in the darkness and rushing with adrenaline, the instinct was simply to point the gun in the right general direction and loose off rounds.

At this point, seeing the threat to the team, the Mk 46 gunner opened up with a long, very long, covering burst of fire that suppressed the PKM gunner and allowed the other SEALs to pull back to more defensible positions, out of the line of fire of both the enemy and of the Mk 48-armed Rangers further back. (Owen notes that the Mk 46 gunner went through an entire 200-round box in one burst, the urgency of the situation overriding the recommended policy of 6–8-round bursts.) Once the SEALs were in cover, they radioed the Rangers for support fire, which they promptly delivered with their Mk 48s, M203 underbarrel grenade launchers, and other weapons. The SEALs used the cover of the fire to radio for close air support, which came three minutes later in an astonishing display of accurate bombing on the tree line.

Following the bombing, the SEALs moved up again to clear the woodland, where they found some dead and wounded Taliban. The SEALs had the tactical support of overhead drone reconnaissance plus the acute senses of a military canine with dog handler; they affectionately called the dog the "hair missile." The drone operator spotted enemy fighters, and highlighted them with the drone's own IR illuminator, so the SEALs could see exactly where their adversaries were. It was a perfect

A US Army Special Forces soldier opens up with his Mk 18 CQBR carbine during a clash in Achin District, Afghanistan, 2016. The weapon is kitted out with an Aimpoint CompM4 red-dot sight, an Insight Technology AN/PEQ-15 ATPIAL, and an Insight Technology WMX200 Visible Bright Light. (US Army photo by Spc Christopher Stevenson)

demonstration of how technology can provide a supreme tactical advantage against a less well-equipped enemy. The dog was also released, and ran up into the trees, found a live enemy fighter, and started to attack him – the screaming Taliban was then dispatched with shots from HK416s.

The SEALs were able to identify a group of five Taliban fighters who had set up a tight defensive position, and who were waiting for the SEALs in the darkness, entirely unaware of how they were actually floodlit by IR light from the drone and now from the SEALs' IR illuminators. The SEALs framed the enemy position with an L-shaped formation, trapping the Taliban fighters in a kill zone. Then the SEALs opened fire. Owen relates how the laser lights danced around and rested on each fighter, at which point the fighters crumpled under the precision fire. Within a matter of seconds, all five fighters were dead and the compound was taken.

Owen is honest in all of his accounts about the sheer psychological confusion and sensory overload of a firefight, even among highly trained SOF troops. Two factors stand out regarding this particular episode, however, from the standpoint of small-arms handling. The first is the significant role of suppressive firepower from the Mk 46 machine gun, which enabled the team to escape to covered positions, and the Mk 48 machine guns further back. This incident unwittingly contributes to the ongoing debate in the US military about the value of belt-felt weapons at squad level. Although the fire from the Mk 46 was undoubtedly far from precise, the duration of the bursts it could deliver provided a suppressive time-window that allowed the other troops to pull back, a feat that would have been far harder to achieve with precision-fire magazine-fed rifles. The other conspicuous advantage the SOF possessed was their IR illuminators, married to NVGs or thermal weapon sights. As the Taliban evidently had (and have) no similar capability, there was an eerie sense of seeing but not being seen; and once the targets were identified they were meticulously lined up for the kill, the enemy being utterly unaware in the darkness that the remaining duration of their lives was being measured out in seconds. It is the capabilities of the weaponry, both machine guns and carbines, which provided the space and orientation for the SEALs to make their tactical maneuvers.

TACTICAL DOMINANCE

We should never ascribe unnecessary influence to any weapon system. Despite the vast technological advantage of the US SOCOM forces in recent conflicts, this does not prevent SOF troops dying as a result of being hit by bursts of less sophisticated AK or PKM fire, or from a talented shot with a basic Dragunov SVD rifle. However, if we assess the outcomes of most combat encounters between US SOF and belligerents, there is a definite sense of a marked disparity in kill ratios. Much of the reason behind this is undoubtedly just better tactical skills. One of the most transparent examples of this in action is the battle of Mogadishu on October 3–4, 1993, when "Task Force Ranger" – a mixed unit of SOCOM forces, weighted mainly toward the men of Bravo Company, 3d Ranger

Battalion, 75th Ranger Regiment, but including soldiers of Delta Force, 160th SOAR, and SEALs – fought a two-day running battle with the irregular troops of Somali warlord Mohamed Farrah Aidid. The numerical disparity between the opposing forces could not have been greater – some 120 US men faced up to 4,000 militiamen and volunteers. (The odds would be evened out somewhat by the later deployment of a large US and UNOSOM rescue force.) By the end of the battle, the US forces had lost 19 dead, 73 wounded, and one captured. By contrast, estimates of enemy casualties (including data from independent agencies) range from *c*.500 up to *c*.1,000. The standard weapons for the Rangers were the conventional 5.56mm M16A2 rifle or the CAR-15 carbine version, typically firing over iron sights and with few extra fittings apart from the M203 underbarrel grenade launcher. Given that the enemy was almost exclusively equipped with AK assault rifles, there was almost nothing in terms of ballistic advantage between the opposing arsenals, although the US troops came to draw upon far heavier fire support from helicopter gunships, vehicle-mounted .50-caliber machine guns, and later armor. One Ranger present in the action remembered, with some disquiet, how he switched from target to target rapidly with his rifle, three or four trigger pulls usually being sufficient to drop and incapacitate (typically kill) an enemy combatant.

Looking at the present day, and especially the period since 2001, we must also give weapon design something of its due. A salient major event in recent SOF history was Operation *Red Wings*, conducted in June–July 2005, which ultimately became the subject of a book and a Hollywood motion picture, both called *Lone Survivor*. The operation occurred in the Pech District of Kunar Province in Afghanistan, and involved the insertion of a four-man SEAL team to conduct covert reconnaissance and surveillance of local Taliban forces. The unit was compromised, and a blistering gunfight developed between the four SEALs and far larger group of Taliban troops, possibly up to 100 in number, armed with machine guns and RPGs as well

Iraq, 2006 (overleaf)

A sniper from the 75th Ranger Regiment, armed with a Mk 11 Mod 0 sniper rifle, provides overwatch as four members of his team advance up a street in Baghdad, 2006. His firearm is set up with the Leupold Mk 4 3.5–10×40 with a Mildot reticle (see inset). The reticle dots are used to calculate distance to targets; they also have the function of aiming points to compensate for holdover and wind drift. Fitted to the front end of the sniper's rifle is an AN/PEQ-2A Advanced Target Pointer/Illuminator/Aiming Light (ATPIAL). The role of this sniper is to provide tactical overwatch as the other team members move forward. Most of the team are equipped with M4A1 Carbines with SOPMOD fittings, including the EOTech 553 HOLOgraphic Weapon Sight (SU-231/PEQ in military designation), the Insight Technology AN/PEQ-15 ATPIAL, and the SU-223/PVS gun light, the illuminator and the light fitted to a dual pressure pad remote switch. On the left, the rear sector is guarded by a Ranger armed with an M249 SAW, with an ELCAN Specter M145 Optical Sight mounted to the top of the receiver. Between them, the unit presents formidable precision and suppressive firepower.

SEAL Team members prior to the ill-fated Operation *Red Wings* in June–July 2005. In this poignant photograph (all but one of the men pictured here were subsequently killed), the team displays its firepower, including a Mk 11 Mod 0 sniper rifle (center) and M4A1 Carbines. (US Navy photo (RELEASED)/Wikimedia/ Public Domain)

as their AK assault rifles. The subsequent battle resulted in three of the SEALs being killed, but not before the SEALs killed more than 30 of the enemy, despite the fact that the Taliban troops had tactical experience. From the account of the action in the book by Marcus Luttrell, one of the SEAL team, we get the impression of the SEALs switching quickly and smoothly between target opportunities, their shooting skills merging with the rapid target acquisition provided by the optical sights on their weapons. The specific weapons carried on the mission were two 5.56mm Mk 12 Mod 1 suppressed SPRs and two M4A1 Carbines mounted with ACOGs and fitted with M203A1 underbarrel grenade launchers.

Despite the harrowing casualties of the mission for the SOF community, including another eight SEALs and eight US Army Special Operations aviators, all of whom were killed when their MH-47 rapid-response helicopter was hit by an RPG and crashed, there is no doubt that in the ground battle the enemy was on an individual basis outclassed both by the skills of the SOF soldiers they faced and the quality of the firearms used.

MV *MAERSK ALABAMA* – SNIPER ACTION

The tactical advantage provided by the SOF community's advanced weaponry also extends to the practice of sniping. The story of the hijacking of the cargo ship MV *Maersk Alabama*, commanded by Captain Richard Phillips, has been immortalized in the motion picture *Captain Phillips*

(2013), with Tom Hanks starring in the eponymous role. The incident was particularly notable for the exceptional talents in marksmanship displayed by a sniper team from SEAL Team Six; looking at the events again we can gain further insight into SOCOM sniping weapons and skills.

Summarizing the lead-up events briefly, on April 8, 2009 four Somali pirates in the Indian Ocean seized the MV *Maersk Alabama* 240 nautical miles southeast of Eyl, Somalia. There followed many hours of increasing tension, with Captain Philips and other crew members being held hostage, while another group of crew members remained hidden, and even managed to secure a pirate hostage of their own. With the situation deteriorating, and the pirates unable to control the modern ship, they eventually fled the *Maersk Alabama* in one of its lifeboats, taking Phillips with them. The US Navy, responding to the crisis, sent the guided-missile destroyer USS *Bainbridge* (DDG-96) and the guided-missile frigate USS *Halyburton* (FFG-40) to the Gulf of Aden, and by April 9 the two warships had closed in on the lifeboat, beginning a tense period of negotiations and threats.

The next day, six SEAL Team Six members flew 16 hours from Oceana, Virginia, to the Somalia coast, and then parachuted covertly into the waters around the standoff. On the night of April 9/10, the situation became even more serious, as a mentally and physically shattered Captain Phillips made an attempt to escape, resulting in a scuffle on the floor of the lifeboat. One of the pirates also fired his AK assault rifle out the back of the lifeboat at the *Halyburton*, effectively clearing the way for the US rescuers to use lethal force. The SEALs embarked on the *Halyburton* on April 11, and transferred to the *Bainbridge* shortly thereafter.

Although this was a sniping mission, the relatively close range of the engagement meant that the SEALs didn't need to bring with them long-

In SOF sniper teams, the spotter is just as vital to the outcome of the shot as the shooter himself. Typical information given by the spotter includes range estimation, target identification, observing environmental effects (wind, heat, etc.), and tactical notes. (Cpl Dean Davis/Wikimedia/Public Domain)

range firepower. Contrary to many reports, which usually ascribe SR-25 semi-automatic DM/sniper rifles as the SEALs' weapons, they were actually equipped with HK416 rifles, fitted with thermal night-vision optics, AAC suppressors, and firing from 16in barrels (Neville 2015). They deployed to the fantail flight deck of the *Bainbridge*, where they could lie flat and carefully study the lifeboat in front of them. The *Bainbridge*'s captain had actually convinced the pirates to allow them to be put under tow, to steady the craft in choppy seas. What this actually achieved was to turn the lifeboat around into a decent firing position for the SEALs, and also to steadily, imperceptibly, draw the lifeboat closer to the warship, until it was about 23m (25yd) off the bow. Nevertheless, the shot profile was demanding: three pirates (another had crossed over to the *Bainbridge*, having been lured with the prospect of negotiating), all armed, in an undulating and partly enclosed lifeboat, and stood within feet of the vulnerable hostage.

On April 12 the SEAL snipers fired near-simultaneous single shots from their HK416 rifles, timing the shots at the precise moment all three pirates showed their heads. The pirates all went down with head shots. Captain Phillips was unharmed. In a notable addition to the action, when other SEALs boarded the lifeboat, they took with them 4.6x30mm MP7 SMGs, and fired multiple shots into the bodies of the three pirates, to ensure that they no longer posed a threat.

From the moment that the hijackers fell under the sights of the snipers, there was a sense that they were doomed. Given that the snipers had fired 5.56mm rounds from the forward deck of the *Bainbridge*, and not hugely destructive rounds of heavier calibers (although we do not know the bullet type that they were using), it was imperative that those shots be delivered with absolute precision if Captain Phillips was to make it out of the lifeboat alive.

CALIBER DEBATES

The selection and configuration of firearms within the SOF community is to some extent dictated by debates about which caliber of weapon is best suited to tactical purposes. This debate can appear arcane to civilian outsiders, but within the military community it is both important and, depending on the forum, frequently heated.

Reducing this debate to its bare essentials, the discussion centers around whether it is better to have a weapon firing a smaller and lighter cartridge – typically the 9x19mm for handguns and the 5.56x45mm for carbines and assault rifles – or beefing-up to heavier cartridges such as the .40 S&W and .45 ACP for handguns and 7.62x51mm NATO for rifles, or some of the new specialist "intermediate" rounds now vying for attention. Multiple factors are part of this discussion, and are slightly different in the context of handguns and long arms, but the positions of advocates of both sides can be summarized as follows.

Advocates for smaller calibers point out that the use of lighter individual cartridges means that the soldier can carry more rounds about

A Scout Sniper fires a Mk 11 Mod 0 sniper rifle, the spent 7.62mm cartridge case ejecting out to the side. Note the dust kick-up; on actual operations the sniper might wet the surrounding earth or spread a cloth over it, to reduce this visual signature. (US DoD by Sgt Alex C. Sauceda)

his person and in his magazines, increasing his firepower. They argue that the lower recoil impulse from smaller calibers improves shot placement on target (accuracy), in both semi-automatic and full-automatic fire modes, by improving recovery between shots. Moreover, the improved controllability of weapons firing smaller calibers means that training times can be reduced, wasting less time teaching the skills of handling recoil. When delivered on-target, smaller calibers have shown they produce the necessary terminal effects to incapacitate the enemy, or to penetrate typical cover. Finally, lighter cartridges are less mechanically punishing than heavier ones, meaning that the weapons that fire them are typically lighter and more compact, improving portability and reducing user fatigue.

Conversely, proponents of heavier calibers argue that such ammunition offers superior terminal ballistics when compared to lighter calibers, producing more decisive incapacitation for fewer rounds fired. Furthermore, heavier calibers, particularly when fired from long-barrel weapons, retain greater kinetic energy and penetration at longer ranges (+457m/500yd). Heavier calibers also promote a better standard of marksmanship, with an emphasis on putting accurate shots on target rather than achieving hits through volume of fire. Finally, heavier calibers have better anti-materiel effects, meaning that it is easier to suppress or incapacitate an enemy behind positions of substantial cover.

Finding a way through this debate is, in reality, not a matter of either/or conclusions. Any military firearm is ultimately an act of compromise, about finding the right weapon to place at the sweet spot in requirements such as budget (including both the cost of the gun and

A US Army Ranger with the 2d Battalion, 75th Ranger Regiment, provides overwatch security with his M249 SAW, fitted with an ELCAN Specter DR scope, during a mission in Iraq, 2006. (Courtesy of US Army Special Operations Command (USASOC)/Wikimedia/Public Domain)

of ammunition), commonality of ammunition supply, training program, typical tactical requirements, and familiarity. Grossly simplifying the outcome of this discussion, however, we can say that on the whole accurate shot placement is now regarded as superior to the terminal ballistic properties of individual cartridges; a small, high-velocity bullet through someone's head, for example, will do far more damage than a very powerful and heavy bullet through an arm. At close to medium ranges, the 9×19mm and 5.56×45mm are both serviceable and potent rounds in handguns and rifles respectively. Beyond ranges of about 549m (600yd), however, operational experience has shown that the 5.56mm round's penetration, energy, and accuracy drop off rapidly compared to that of 7.62mm cartridges. Thus in a long-range gun battle, as has been commonly experienced in Afghanistan, the side with heavier calibers of weaponry tends to hold the advantage, at least in a straightforward exchange of fire.

The discussion is now no longer a matter of 5.56mm vs 7.62mm, however. At the time of writing, intensive trials, investigations, and arguments are being conducted to establish the merits of various new calibers, e.g. 6.5mm Creedmoor; 6.5mm Grendel; 6.8mm Special Purpose Cartridge; .300 AAC Blackout. What each of these cartridges offer, their advocates claim, is superior penetration and range over the practical combat distances from CQB up to 914m (1,000yd), thus filling the range gap many commentators and troops perceived during combat in Afghanistan. It is this debate about caliber, plus bullet design, that is likely to influence the prospective development of SOCOM firearms – but that is just part of the future of SOCOM weaponry.

CONCLUSION

What we can see over more than three decades of SOCOM weapon acquisition and development, is an attempt to find a near-perfect synchronicity between human being and firearm. Human beings, with a little good training, can be excellent shots with even the most basic of weapons; US sharpshooters, for example, were taking kills out to several hundred yards during the American Revolutionary War of the 18th century, using muzzle-loaded rifled muskets and nothing more than the most basic of iron sights. The SOCOM weapons and accessories, however, take good firearms skills and maximize their potential exponentially, through the use of advanced optics, targeting technologies, materiel technologies, and ergonomic advances. The levels of innovation in SOCOM weapons programs have been constant and restless, the weapon-program managers and the SOF troops themselves always on the lookout for a configuration or firearm that will give them the fractional advantages in combat that could mean the difference between living or dying.

We have already acknowledged that modularity and accessorization have been two of the guiding forces behind SOCOM firearms development. These trends will continue unabated, as will the explorations of caliber noted above. (The May 2018 online edition of *Military Times* featured an article entitled "SOCOM snipers will ditch their bullets for this new round next year," the writer revealing that the new round is the 6.5mm Creedmoor.) Yet arguably the real future, the true revolution, in the military firearms of SOCOM will come in the form of the deeper integration between weapon and computerized fire-control systems. In 2011, for example, the TrackingPoint company revealed a new precision-guided firearm system with a sight that features an advanced ballistic calculator and tracking system. When the shooter spots a target, he simply designates the target roughly by squeezing the trigger halfway, at which point the Networked Tracking Scope tracks the target and calculates the

A screenshot from the heads-up display of a TrackingPoint Precision Guided Firearm. The sight has now locked onto the target, having calculated all the relevant range and ballistic information. (Oren Schauble/ Wikimedia/CC BY-SA 3.0)

range and the ballistic solution. The crosshairs of the scope then lock onto the target, and the shooter pulls the trigger fully; but the weapon will not actually fire until it is perfectly aligned, and a hit is guaranteed – total time-to-kill is about 2.5 seconds, even for a rapidly moving target. Basically, the system gives the shooter the capability of an elite marksman with only a fraction of the training. TrackingPoint has already mounted the sight on a variety of 5.56mm, 7.62mm, and .300 Blackout weapons, and the military has been conducting its own internal trials since 2014.

Similarly, the Small Arms Ammunition Configuration study released in 2017 has led some to suggest that the future of firearms lies in weapons that fire small high-velocity darts, but guided to the target through a computerized fire-control connected to a heads-up display; the shooter would not even need to physically look down a sight to aim and fire the weapon, meaning he could shoot around or over cover without exposing himself.

Another major area of future discussion is the type of weapons in the SOF team or squad. There is a general interest in replacing both the carbine and the LMG with a single weapon, one that offers better range and on-target effects than the carbine and more precision than the LMG. This shift has already been practically expressed in the US Marine Corps' adoption of the 5.56×45mm M27 Infantry Automatic Rifle (IAR), based on the HK416, and is a core discussion in the US Army's Next Generation Squad Weapon program, which, it is hoped, will bring a new weapon type into the field by 2022.

It is impossible to divine what technology will bring over the next 30 years of SOCOM's existence. Suffice to say that the US SOF community has in many ways been a driving force in small-arms technology, in their relentless search for the perfect tactical weapon. As potential enemies evolve, both irregular and conventional, this search will continue.

BIBLIOGRAPHY

Bowden, Mark (2000). *Black Hawk Down*. London: Corgi.

Department of Defense (2009). *Dictionary of Military and Associated Terms*: Washington, DC: Department of Defense.

Department of the Army (1993). *An Infantryman's Guide to Combat in Built-Up Areas.* Washington, DC: Headquarters, Department of the Army.

Crane, David (2011). "The SCAR Program: Present and Future." Available at: https://www.americanrifleman.org/articles/2011/2/17/the-scar-program-present-and-future/

Erickson, Karl (2016). "When to use Night Vision | IR Illuminators | Tactical Rifleman." YouTube. Available at: https://www.youtube.com/watch?v=ocmaUxEfZrc&t=320s

Gurwitch, Jeff (2011). "Tactical Rifle Slings for Close Quarters Battle/Close Quarters Combat (CQB/CQC) and Tactical 3-Gun Competition Applications: Finding the Right One for You!" Defensereview.com. Available at: http://www.defensereview.com/tactical-rifle-slings-for-close-quarters-battleclose-quarters-combat-cqbcqc-and-tactical-3-gun-competition-applications-finding-the-right-one-for-you/

Haney, Eric L. (2003). *Inside Delta Force: The Story of America's Elite Counterterrorist Unit.* London: Transworld.

Luttrell, Marcus (with Patrick Robinson) (2014). *Lone Survivor*. London: Sphere.

Markham, George (1995). *Guns of the Elite: Special Forces Firearms, 1940 to the Present.* London: Arms & Armour.

Neville, Leigh (2008). *Special Operations Forces in Afghanistan*. Elite 163. Oxford: Osprey Publishing.

Neville, Leigh (2008). *Special Operations Forces in Iraq*. Elite 170. Oxford: Osprey Publishing.

Neville, Leigh (2015). *Guns of the Special Forces*. Barnsley: Pen & Sword.

Neville, Leigh (2015). *Special Forces in the War on Terror*. Oxford: Osprey Publishing.

Neville, Leigh (2018). *Modern Snipers*. Oxford: Osprey Publishing.

Owen, Mark (2014). *No Hero: The Evolution of a Navy SEAL*. New York, NY: Penguin.

Plaster, Major John M. (2006). *The Ultimate Sniper: An Advanced Training Manual for Military and Police Snipers*. Boulder, CO: Paladin Press.

Pushies, Fred (2016). *US Special Ops: The History, Weapons, and Mission of Elite Military Forces.* Minneapolis, MN: Voyageur Press.

Raymond, Adam (2017). "'We Own the Night': The Rise And Fall Of The US Military's Night-Vision Dominance." *Task & Purpose*. Available at: https://taskandpurpose.com/night-rise-fall-us-militarys-night-vision-dominance

Schgol, Jeff (2017). "As enemy body armor improves, Marines test new bullets." *Marine Corps Times*. Available at: https://www.marinecorpstimes.com/news/your-marine-corps/2017/06/08/as-enemy-body-armor-improves-marines-test-new-bullets/

South, Todd (2018). "SOCOM snipers will ditch their bullets for this new round next year." *Military Times*. Available at: https://www.militarytimes.com/news/your-military/2018/05/08/socom-snipers-will-ditch-their-bullets-for-this-new-round-next-year/

Taylor, Gus (2005). "SOPMOD Program Overview" (PPT presentation). SOPMOD Program Manager.

US Special Operations Command (2009). "Precision Sniper Rifle (PSR)." Solicitation Number: H92222-09-PSR2. Available at: https://www.fbo.gov/index?s=opportunity&mode=form&id=8d443a1c66be88df1e9f29112e711e8a&tab=core&_cview=0&cck=1&au=&ck=

INDEX